EMMA WOOD was born in Yorkshire in 1958. She stayed on in East Anglia after reading History at Cambridge University. She did a variety of jobs after graduating including TEFL and washing-up in college kitchens. She finished up as partner in a junk stall which traded on markets throughout the area. She moved from Norfolk to Sutherland in 1987 and after two years went to Ross-shire where she now lives on the delightful Heights of Achterneed. She teaches English and creative writing, and is a freelance editor and writer. She is writing a book of short stories and is planning a study on *Change in the Highlands since 1945*.

She has one daughter, Jasmine.

Notes from the North
incorporating
a brief history of the Scots and the English

EMMA WOOD

Luath Press Limited
EDINBURGH
www.luath.co.uk

First Edition 1998

The paper used in this book is recyclable. It is made from low chlorine
pulps produced in a low energy, low emission manner
from renewable forests.

Printed and bound by
Caledonian International Book Manufacturing Ltd., Glasgow

Typeset in 10.5 point Sabon by
S. Fairgrieve, Edinburgh, 0131 658 1763

For Jasmine and Lucy

I have caught the slow train that stops everywhere - Darlington, Durham, Newcastle, meandering its way along the Northumberland coast to Berwick. As we cross the Tweed the air seems to lighten and the sky begins to dry a little and, like a watermark, the pale sheen of a rainbow welcomes our train over the border. I'm in another country, the one called home.

from *Behind the Scenes at the Museum* by Kate Atkinson

The Highlands of Scotland in the late 1840s were convulsed by the social disintegration and severe economic hardship produced chiefly by the Highland Clearances which had been underway for half a century.

In 1842, in Ross-shire, the circumstances of the enforced removal of the people of Glencalvie attracted the attention of the national press. In 1846, potato blight struck a year after its disastrous appearance in Ireland. The Highlanders were as dependent on potatoes as the Irish and famine ensued. In 1847, the situation was still desperate and food riots were occurring throughout the Highlands. In 1848, Queen Victoria and Prince Albert visited Deeside for the first time. The Queen recorded the enchantment both felt in her diary:

It was so clear and solitary, it did one good as one gazed round; and the pure mountain air was most refreshing. All seemed to breathe freedom and peace, and to make one forget the world and its sad turmoils.

Contents

Preface

THE MOST IMPORTANT STATEMENT which must preface all I have to say is that my discussion of the peoples of England and Scotland is dedicated to explaining and understanding the difference between them as opposed to committing, even accidentally, the racist offence of identifying in them any sort of inherent characteristic as a basis for otherness. Rather, I have tried to use the geography of these islands and as much of their history as possible to account for those differences which undoubtedly do exist between the two nations.

I must also warn readers not to expect a rigorously empirical study supported at every turn by concrete evidence. My expertise is not in researching this field with sociological exactness, but in being English in the Highlands over the last ten years. This meant knowing what it was like during the two General Elections won by the Tories despite the remoteness of their policies from Scotland's preoccupations and the scarcity of Tory MPs there. Now, of course, it's New Labour and its Devolution programme; but this book has to stop somewhere and as I hope that Devolution will mean a radically fresh start in Scotland's relations with England, I have chosen to end with the Devolution Referendum on 11 September 1997.

Inevitably then, in the book's mix of subjectivity and objectivity, subjectivity does rather well for itself. But I can assure readers there is no partiality towards English or Scots or towards any political party. My only bias is towards a mere idea which has emerged from a long and detailed look into the historical relationship between Scotland and England, from before the time the two regions knew themselves as separate countries, up to the present potential watershed in their relationship that is New Labour's Devolution Referendum. This idea makes the simple claim that if Scotland and England were able to relate to one another and the rest of the world more as sovereign equals and less as squabbling siblings, the resulting benefit would be substantial for the relationship between the English and Scots wherever they find themselves.

I started thinking about writing this book in 1993 when the chances of constitutional reform looked impossibly remote. So did, therefore, the advent of any change in the *modus vivendi* of the two ancient, feuding neighbours. What follows is an account of my own personal search for an understanding of how such a monumentally unproductive situation has arisen and what remedy, if any, exists for it.

No doubt what follows will prove to contain too many subjective generalisations for the taste of some readers. All I can offer them is the assurance that I have followed the example of many of my Scottish friends' consistent refusal to say *amen* to any assertion without subjecting it to the severest scrutiny possible.

Now we look forward to a Scottish Assembly and all that it promises for a constructive reworking of the old attitudes of England and Scotland to each other. As part of this realignment there is a pressing need for English ignorance about Scotland, her peoples and history to end. I want to see a decline in such ignorance especially amongst those English people who choose to settle in Scotland. Only when the English are more fully aware of Scottish issues and the background to them will they realise how important it is for the future political arrangements between the two countries to be fair and just, thus escaping completely from the chill shadow of medieval power politics. I hope that whatever form such arrangements take, a state of justice and equality will be attained. But for this outcome to be achieved, and for it to endure, such ignorance must cease and it is to that end that this book has been written.

I thank everyone who has helped in the writing of this book

and especially all my interviewees; also, Nellie Pickering, Liz Gordon, Dot Jessiman, Fiona Robertson and the staff at Dingwall Library, Sadie MacLeod, Julie MacWilliam, Julia and Scott Russell, Bill Griffin, Ali Smith, Vic Gatrell, Nancy Kinloch, Jem Taylor, Marj Donaldson, the Collie Effect, Rod and Pat Richard, Paul Mounsey for *Nahoo* and the inspiration of all my friends in Scotland and England. I especially thank Rob Gibson for his helpful scrutiny of the Brief History. Any mistakes, however, are all my own.

Emma Wood
November 1998

CHAPTER I

Comparisons are Odious but...

IT'S SEPTEMBER 1982 AND I'm up on holiday in the Highlands as has now become usual and necessary. Load van up with bedding and cooking gear and head north, the ultimate direction. Simple guarantee of pure perfection as expressed by distance from London, capital hub of an élitist and increasingly irresponsible state.

It had been a tense spring and summer in England. In April, the Argentinians had invaded the Falkland Islands long ago lost to the British Empire. Jorge Luis Borges is reported to have likened the ensuing military conflict between Britain and Argentina to 'two bald men fighting over a comb'. I shared his contempt for such ludicrous behaviour and I was afraid that the foolishness could have dark consequences if the nuclear weapons which the euphemistically named British Task Force had taken to the South Atlantic hit the fan accidentally or otherwise. All in all, it was a shameful time. *The Sun* sold millions of newspapers foaming suddenly respectable obscenities about 'Argy-bargy' and worse. It was Thatcher's finest hour. She mesmerised most of the official opposition into supine agreement with her absurd re-run of 19th century gunboat diplomacy and laid the foundations of what would be a new record majority in the Parliamentary elections of the following year.

I remember meeting a good old Norfolk boy (a farm labourer who could have been almost any age apart from that of a boy) whilst out on my pushbike one May afternoon. The whole Malvinas business had gone so far that the mixture of shame and dread it inspired hung over my enjoyment of the May-time hedgerows like a nasty smell. As I rode home from the village shop, I was hailed from the verge by Soot who was clearing out a drain. He had always

1

worked on farms and had never lived outside the parish. He'd been given his name when, as a lad, he'd solved the crisis of having no white paint to mark out the football pitch by successfully substituting soot. He was a jovial and kindly man, always ready for a good gossip preferably washed down with a cup of tea or a pint of bitter. I loved the way his automatic reaction to any pain or difficulty, including his own, was to throw back his white head and shout out laughter. At such moments I would silently salute him as a Zen peasant and feel proud to know him. But that afternoon, as we stood together in the middle of the tiny Norfolk road, my veneration came unstuck. We got on to the Argies and Soot's solution was simple: 'Nook (remember how Bernard Matthews says 'Boo-iful') the blerdy lo'. Thass what Oi'd do,' he declared. He was utterly serious despite his customary guffaw. I saw there was no point in debating the ethical or practical implications of his idea just as there had never been the slightest chance of constructive debate with Soot about organic farming, forgiving the Germans or the myriad shortcomings of the Tory Party. I was used to his intransigence but I was still shocked by the ignorant arrogance with which Soot could even half imagine such a course of action. It was too close to what frightened me to laugh it off. Happily the British government didn't adopt Soot's plan, but I knew as he said it that plenty of people thought like him and probably said so before June 14, when the Argentinian soldiers on the Falklands surrendered.

The September of the same year saw me delightedly tramping over the hills which overlooked the Pentland Firth on Scotland's north coast. One hundred and seventy-five years earlier, inhabitants of the fertile valley of Strathnaver, which I could just see inland to the west, had been summarily evicted by the agents of the Duchess of Sutherland, their chieftain and landlord whom they called Ban Mhorair Chataibh, Great Lady of Sutherland. She and her advisers provided little assistance to the dispossessed tenants of Strathnaver as they struggled for subsistence on the barren and alien shore. They had been removed from their homes to make way for sheep walks which promised to yield the Great Lady a substantial rise in the cash income she received from these stony acres. The Duchess and her advisers had no more considered asking her tenantry if such a proposal was to their liking in 1807 than I had any idea why these stunning green hills were almost empty of people in 1982.

I sat on a hill-top which was riddled with sandy rabbit holes and ate my lunch. I was enchanted by the jagged horizons to the mountainous west and by the seething Pentland Firth and hazily distant Orkney Islands straight ahead. There was silence, apart from the occasional sheep bleat and constant bird calls, and the air, cool despite the noon-day sun, was deliciously fresh and clear. ML appeared from beneath my vantage point. He was riding a quad-bike and had a pair of glasses hanging from his neck fastened to a piece of orange bailer-twine. He looked as if he'd spent most of his life in the open air and he smiled so that I knew it was fine for me to be sitting there eating my sandwiches. He got off the bike, said hello and settled down for a chat. I was delighted. I had lots to ask about the landscape, flowers and birds and the Beast of Skerra which was rumoured to be prowling those very hills that year. ML was a local crofter and I knew I had an expert on hand. I revelled in the richness of the environment he was explaining as he answered my questions in the delightfully soft sing-song of the north Highlands. But it wasn't all one-way traffic. He wanted to know where I belonged (nowhere, but I live in Norfolk); what were the farms like there; how did most people earn a living. Inevitably, we talked about politics and, as a polite guest, I avoided airing any views which might cause offence. I needn't have worried: he was as determined an anti-Thatcherite as I was and his gently-spoken, simple verdict on the heroine of the South Atlantic, who most of

England was still hoarse from cheering, was music to my ears. 'What a dreadful, dreadful woman,' he exclaimed in quiet tones of mystified horror. I wanted, for a mad moment, to hug him: to come all the way to this heavenly spot and find someone, almost part of the landscape, ready to condemn the woman who seemed to have most of England in her dreary thrall. But there was nothing we could do about her right then so I finished my sandwich and he got back on his bike and roared off to gather his sheep down by the shore. Even there in radiant Sutherland I knew not all Scots felt the same as ML. But what a fantastic difference from dear old Soot!

In 1997 only 25% of the Scottish electorate voted for the Tory Party and its championing of the Union. By this time I had learned enough about the Scottish history of the last millennium to know exactly why most Scots had little reason to want the *status quo* maintained. Fifteen years after meeting ML, I'm convinced that this grass roots anti-authoritarianism is one of the biggest differences between English and Scottish society. History, from the broadsword to the ballot box, has given the Scots good reason to question the decisions of Southern authority and to take the pretensions of that authority less than seriously.

CHAPTER 2

Tribes, Communities and Commuters

MARKET FORCES HAVE HI-JACKED the adjective 'natural' for a variety of verbal prostitutions: 'natural fragrance' normally refers to chemically produced perfumes; 'natural flavour' almost always describes processed food and so-called 'natural materials' often turn out to be synthetic in origin. So 'natural' is terminally devalued as a term of reference. However, there is surely one use which we can justify quite pragmatically: communities are natural arenas for the development of human society. To survive and endure as a species, humans must reproduce and this cannot be done in isolation. A study of almost intact aboriginal communities in the Amazon Forest show how child-rearing practices, when located firmly in the tribe, work with apparently Utopian consequences. Jean Liedloff, the author of this study (*The Continuum Concept*, Penguin Books, 1989) claims persuasively that this success is based on the way these tribe-based practices meet the precise and varying needs of the developing human child. The children studied by Liedloff are looked after by the whole community in ways which result in their becoming perfectly adapted to fulfilling the needs of that community. Before they can walk the children are carried by their parents as they go about their grown-up business. Once the children are old enough to walk they are automatically and fully involved in the life of the tribe either helping adults with miniature knives or tools (definitely not toys) or being watched over with their peers by the tribe's older children. Thus are they prepared indirectly but comprehensively for the later roles they will go on to assume in the tribe. These customary practices are cause and effect in the creation of a spectacularly functional communal effort in which all members, regardless of age, are involved and perfectly qualified to be involved. The resulting society is surely natural in that it operates without reliance on or reference to civilised values or agenda or non-indigenous factors of any kind. It also shows just how much a truly functional community provides for every one of its members.

'Natural' has probably been misused most spectacularly in the sentimentalised worship of The Past: if something happened in the past it is somehow desirable. This is quite wrong. Life in the past was unmistakably nasty, brutish and short. Life expectancy alone as comparatively late as the 19th century is quite enough to shatter our soft-focus delusions about the good old days. I would contend, however, that there was at least one thing good about the past. By good I mean better than the present and by the past I mean before the various radical changes which affected society with the coming of the Industrial Revolution and its substitution of human rhythms by mechanical ones. Whole academic careers have been spent on the macro-controversy: Was the Industrial Revolution a Good or a Bad Thing? A variety of economic indices constitutes the ammunition for both sides: wages, working conditions, crime, education, infant mortality and life expectancy. Yet what the Industrial Revolution did, and what the market, as first identified by the Liberal economists of the 18th and 19th century, did wherever people experienced it, was to destroy communities. The consequences of this destruction are hard to quantify in the way one can do for the other countables already mentioned. The negative effects of damaged communities are not only confined to the past: news broadcasts remind us constantly that our society is still dominated by such changes. We have unquestionably become a generally insecure society surrounded by strangers and beset by perceived dangers. Family break-up, crime, the alienation which results in routine and widespread drug abuse and environmental degradation (planet abuse) are powerful indicators of the fact that communities have been fatally weakened everywhere. State agencies attempting to remedy an outbreak of any of these social ills often treat the re-establishment or nurturing of community networks as a priority, as evidenced in the promotion of the Neighbourhood Watch Schemes and self-help groups.

No doubt some historians arguing for the fundamentally beneficial nature of the Industrial Revolution have identified significant trends of geographical and social mobility in existence before the Industrial Revolution. However, it is certain that at the end of the First World War, communities the length and breadth of the developed world had already begun to experience a gradual process of terminal decline. Indicators of this decline include the growth of anonymity between adjacent households and a reduction in effective support systems other than, or perhaps even including, those of close kinship. The chronology is quite straightforward. From the mid-18th to mid-19th century the new manufacturing industries' demand for labour all over Britain created a mass exodus from the countryside. Communities were born in the new urban areas whose recently assembled inhabitants did not know how to live in any other way. The communal working patterns of pre-industrial agriculture were replaced by the shared experience of the factory. People on the whole tended to stay in the same place and do the same job during their lifetimes. After two centuries, however, important changes have occurred. One is the irreversible decline of many major British industries. This process was underway after the First World War and intensified after the Second. The communities which existed only because these industries did, could not outlast them except as ghosts, robbed of purpose and meaning. Mrs Thatcher, whether symptom or cause, presided over a radically violent chapter of this disintegration in employment patterns which occurred from the early 1980s onwards. It is now expected of those lucky enough to be employed at all to move anywhere in Britain or even across the world to do their bosses' bidding. Contracts in many types of employment are very often temporary or part-time or both. The victims of the Thatcher era also include those not lucky enough to have a job at all. Monetarist policies demolished many working communities by destroying their focal points. Mines, factories and whole industrial complexes have disappeared leaving behind, in the place of self-sufficient, strongly functional communities, desolation, alienation and despair.

Grimethorpe, a former mining town in South Yorkshire is no longer renowned for the health of its community relations, its low crime rate and its prize-winning brass band. Since the pit was closed down there, male unemployment is as high as 80% - 90% in some pockets and the town's new reputation is as a centre for heroin addiction. Ex-miners find '*brown*', as they call the drug, is cheaper and more effective than beer. Children with no hope of finding employment locally are said to be experimenting with heroin at twelve or thirteen. This tragic example is an extreme case of a single, commonplace event, the collapse of a community's strengths and values following the destruction of its primary function. Few places in the industrial West can be certain of immunity from this sort of occurrence.

The Industrial Revolution is not only crucially important to the history of communities in the British Isles because of the wholly new way it organised production. Ultimately it also led to fundamental changes in society through the very commodities it produced. It is in the nature of the unprecedentedly radical changes begun by the Industrial Revolution that its seemingly modest beginnings in the textile manufacture of 18th century Coalbrookdale led to global communications, space exploration, key-hole surgery, computer dating and... all the rest of our technological riches. One of those developments which affected people and communities across the world most profoundly was the invention of the internal combustion engine and the subsequent world-wide expansion of the motor manufacturing industry. Cars are now so mundane and ubiquitous that it is almost possible to overlook the changes wrought on Western society by them from the early 1960s. Since then, major social and economic developments have occurred which could only have taken place against a background of mass car ownership. One of the most socially revolutionary of these changes is the phenomenal rise of commuting. The car has made it possible for vast numbers of people to live in one place (often relatively rural) and work for a living in another (often relatively urban). As a result the British Isles are covered with extraordinarily schizophrenic settlements which are more or less deserted during office hours but come alive with all the technological trappings of contemporary affluence at night and at weekends. Mothers or (less usually) fathers with pre-school children are among the few inhabitants of such settlements to be seen during weekdays. In fact, the desirable norm for modern parents is to get back to work as soon as they can, so there is a sense that these parents at home in the quiet of the working day are only temporarily stranded away from where the real action is. The other group which inhabits these places for more than evenings and weekends is retired people who may well arrive having spent their working lives somewhere else. The most constant residents, the regulars on any roster of daily presence are, therefore, parents of small children, by definition, a somewhat preoccupied group and old people who may well have no working links with the area. The commuter settlement is thus an anti-focal point which can flourish as a functional entity only with the assistance of resources, activities and skills from elsewhere. Its strength as a community is seriously restricted by a lack of shared function and focus.

Rural communities never recovered from the first radical

changes which the Agricultural and Industrial Revolutions wrought on employment and community patterns. Agribusiness shapes the countryside now and has the same crushing imperatives as industry. Massive factory farms are run by very few workers using big machines and lots of chemicals. Planting and harvesting decisions will soon be made on the basis of satellite-generated information. More to the present point are the social results of these developments on the countryside. The steep decline in the number of agricultural jobs brought on by the advent of ultra-modern mechanised farming has left the countryside more than ever bereft of inhabitants who work where they live. It has become in fact an empty place ripe for take-over by developments catering for commuters.

Early in the course of the Industrial Revolution the tendency of industrialists and entrepreneurs to quit the scene of their commercial triumphs as quickly as economically possible was typical. The sort of class consciousness that was at the root of this aversion to living over the shop is no longer a major motivation for the commuter lifestyle. The Victorians justified their choices to flee from the urban setting of the manufacturing industry by stressing the benefits of country living, away from the hurly burly of the business place. Early this century politicians, planners and developers became convinced of these benefits. The resulting construction of new towns and commuter settlements combined with the appearance of affordable motor cars to cause an unprecedented shift away from the idea that work and home are situated in roughly the same geographical space. This trend is not the social mobility of the 19th century when labour followed employment and then stayed put unless there were compelling economic reasons for it to do otherwise. The last thirty to forty years have seen something historically unique: the emergence of a rootless majority who have small need to know their neighbours and whose kin is visitable (by car or public transport) but is in day-to-day terms remote. Such widespread social isolation, such minimal community, would have been unthinkable to the inhabitants of these islands as recently as one hundred years ago.

In contemporary society, most homes whether physically separate or not, very rarely share a common occupational or functional concern. The major shared characteristic of commuter dwellings is in the significant distance they are from their inhabitants' workplaces. More or less meaningful relationships may endure in this half-world where individuals are only ever partly themselves because the work they do in order to survive happens somewhere else. Our society consistently defines its members in terms of how they earn their living. Yet their most important piece of territory, home, is not the place where they create the wealth to support the panoply of comfort which constitutes that home.

To any time-traveller coming from a pre-industrial age, our contemporary commuter settlements would be, on an average weekday, a silent though opulent mystery. There would be no signs of productive activity, no people, no useful animals, no noise and all doors locked tightly against nobody. Even in the evenings and at weekends our time-traveller would be able to see little evidence of purposeful human contact between families in the commuter village. The resulting communities are, therefore, merely *de facto* arithmetical coincidences: groups of people whose only significant shared attribute is their sleeping place, their dormitory. Plenty of scope for squabbling about the village equivalent of the bedclothes, that is noise levels, boundaries, access rights and a hundred other infuriations which are pathetically petty until it's you who's involved in one. That such squabbles can loom so large in commuter communities may well be because such communities have no form of shared, positive purpose beyond mere residence. Commuter villagers don't know their neighbours through knowing or experiencing what they do. The distant jobs done away from the village are many and various but this diversity is not translated into daily reality in the commuter settlement. There, everyone does the same: relax privately in different ways and make as good as possible his or her escape from work. There is, therefore, no diversity and a minimal sense of belonging to anything particularly meaningful.

It should be clear from all I've said that I see the disappearance of meaningful community in our modern world as a major human tragedy. I'm well aware that the communities of the past could be claustrophobic, authoritarian and narrow-minded, but even with such serious flaws, communities could give their members a sense of shared purpose and accountability. That modern Western society provides no sense of a common purpose beyond 'getting and spending' must, in part at least, be connected to much that plagues that society: institutionalised crime and vandalism, widespread drug addiction, family break-up and a general sense of *anomie*. Most compelling of all is the paradox between the tragedy of contemporary lack of meaningful community and the apparent luxury of our current freedom of movement. The movers that typify this luxury have a central part in this book. They are the life-style refugees who change places not because they have to but because they want to. The widespread existence of ghost commuter villages relates to this experience in two ways.

First, to leave your home, friends, family and familiar surroundings for anything less imperative than dire economic necessity presupposes a lack of meaningful connection with the society these life-style refugees are prepared to abandon. Second, to arrive midway (roughly) through your life in a place where you have no history and must construct your own future presupposes the existence of communities where proof of a useful function is not necessarily a compulsory entrance requirement. When John Guthrie arrives at his new home, Kinraddie, in Lewis Grassic Gibbon's

Sunset Song, set in Aberdeen-shire shortly before World War I, his occupation fits neatly into a pre-existing collective of experience and expectation. He has come from a farming community very similar to Kinraddie and can, therefore, assume his position in this new place without any locals-versus-newcomers tension being mentioned at all. Lewis Grassic Gibbon wrote *Sunset Song* in part at least as a lament for the passing of a way of life based on small-scale unmechanised farming which began to disappear after World War I. There was a heterogeneity in society, especially rural society, before the First World War which is unimaginable today. Its disappearance and the converse growth in both individual rootlessness and meaningless settlements are essential preconditions for this modern counter-stream migration, that is migration inspired by the wish for a change in lifestyle rather than specific economic imperatives. So, because of the nature of the society which contained both his origins and destination, John Guthrie belonged in Kinraddie as soon as he arrived there. Few contemporary arrivals will be likely to make such a smooth transition.

1956-1996: My Town

Let me tell you about the place where I, someone who did change places, grew up. I'm not claiming it as uniquely interesting but exactly the opposite: it is a typical example of a dormitory settlement without community, a settlement based on proximity, a mere aggregation of strangers. My parents, anticipating the arrival of children, decided to move out of Leeds in 1956. They had no connections with the village which they chose as home. When I asked my mother recently why they had moved away from the city where they had both grown up and where my father's family still lived she replied with all the vague subjectivity of real humanity over sociological statistic: 'We wanted to move to the country: we had no garden in Headingley. My father worked as a solicitor in Leeds, my mother stayed at home and looked after me. Once in the village, they didn't go to church or take part in any village activities apart from my dad playing in the local cricket team. They were not joiners, their close ties were with friends and family outwith the village. I grew up knowing the shopkeepers and their staff but few other village residents. Even my school friends were not local as I was sent to a private prep school which many pupils came some distance to attend. This isolation from my peers was confirmed for good when my mother, now widowed, scraped together the money to send me to private boarding school in genteel (in parts) Harrogate, twelve miles away. This rejection of the local comprehensive at Tadcaster put the seal on my failure ever to become part of what community there was where my parents had chosen for my sake to settle.

1996

The first overwhelming impression is the number and speed of cars and lorries on the High Street, the main and only road through the village. I can imagine future generations amazed at the casual juxtaposition of family shoppers with these hurtling, toxic dangers. There has been talk of zebra crossings and a bypass since my childhood when the traffic was much lighter. Neither of these has happened although the volume of traffic has increased to the point where there is absolutely nothing to be gained by a visit to the village more than the shopping or services you came for. The High Street is full of fumes and noise. The speed of the traffic is quite frightening, especially for the elderly or parents of small children. There are similar changes in the details of the place. Of course as I am now unmistakably middle-aged, it is inevitable that the shopkeepers of my youth should have been replaced by a new cast. However, the significant change is not one of personnel but of the shops' own identities. The grocer's shop where my mother had her choice of cheese cut and her bacon sliced has been replaced by a self-service outlet: part of one of the franchised chains with branches everywhere in the country which are out of easy reach of a major supermarket. My mother and I knew Mr and Mrs Ryder, who owned and ran the shop when I was little, and their assistants well enough to be quite familiar with their daily concerns, like Mary's shingles, Annie's grand-daughter starting school and Mr and Mrs Ryder's son training to be an accountant in Leeds. There was time for these modest relationships while they sliced the bacon or cut the cheese onto greaseproof paper or reached packets or bottles for us from the shelves behind the long marble counter. Now shopping at any of these outlets is a question of filling your basket from the silent shelves and presenting it to whichever part-time, poorly-paid employee happens to be on the till at the time. The manager is in the background conducting all-important communications with the omnipotent head office rather than forming a relationship with his customers. The general unsatisfactoriness of this set-up is reinforced by the certain knowledge that everything you have chosen could be bought more cheaply at a superstore in any of the nearby larger towns. Indeed in semi-rural areas like this the haves and have-nots in the important terms of shopping opportunities are defined quite simply according to car-ownership. There is now a huge Co-op superstore in nearby Wetherby but the money-saving weekly shop there is only a public transport option for the physically fit unencumbered by small children. Ryder's replacement is a cramped and grimy shopping ghetto for those denied access to the flashier expanses of the distant, cheaper superstores.

What other changes in the village since my childhood in the early 1960s? Well, the library is now a travel agent's and the encyclopaedic hardware/gardening shop is the site of an exclusive (euphemism meaning too expensive for most of the people who actually live round here) clothes shop. The doctor's surgery has moved from its central position to purpose-built neo-classical premises a long way from the shops: another destination best suited to those in good physical shape travelling without too many children and of course to those with access to a car. Both the newsagents have turned from businesses run by local families to branches of national chains. Again, the imposing counter has gone as well as the shadowy recesses, prohibited but tantalisingly full of possibilities. Even removing my nostalgically rose-tinted glasses I cannot detect a superior or even equivalent range of goods for sale. The haberdasher's is now a building society, one of the two fish and chip shops is a Chinese take-away. Mr and Mrs Lawson's chemist shop is a restaurant which has incorporated the old chemist's fittings in its decor. The previously very utilitarian post office has become a gift and card shop: a tasteful setting for cashing your giro. Despite the building of lots of new houses there are no new schools. As if to deny that all these fabulous new fascias really denote the achievement of general progress, at the west end of the village the large primary school is still housed in the post-war prefabs which were just a temporary measure in 1960.

My parents rejected life in the city because it was too big and busy to feel like home. Yet after nearly forty years, almost a lifetime of residence in the village, my mother chose, on the grounds of financial common sense, to leave the village altogether. There seemed, once her calculations were done, nothing to keep her from leaving the village, no relationships to regret, no networks to unpick. She moved to Harrogate and now she lives in a row of 1960s flats where the neighbouring households are a mystery to her and, it seems, to each other.

All of which, *via* my parents' individual connections to Jewish

Poland, Edwardian Darlington, the Australia which mourned Gallipoli and the comfortable merchant class of the West Riding of Yorkshire, only goes to show how rootless I and many of my generation are who came from all over the place to nowhere in particular. Born in the age of the motor car, I grew up in a place which was not home to my parents, their parents, any of their family, or, inevitably, to me.

I once heard some member of the chattering classes say on one of those programmes which pay people to make such assertions, that everyone feels there is something distinctive about the place in which he or she grew up. Yet I believe that a sense of belonging to somewhere special because it's the place which belongs to us is fast becoming a rare thing. The man on the radio was no chicken; if he'd been younger I suspect he wouldn't have made such a genera-lisation. I'm certainly not cataloguing these details of my home town out of the slightest sense of its singularity. Rather it is a sample of much I have seen throughout Britain and which I have every reason to expect prevails elsewhere in the developed economies. The truth is not that my village is unique but inevitably the same as everywhere else. The focus of its inhabitants as they produce and consume has shifted right out of the village. It is no longer self-sufficient even in terms of what you can buy in the shops. By the time I was in my teens, I had learnt the dismal basics of not belonging to it.

So, what do you do and where do you go to do it when home doesn't feel like anywhere special? Incomers everywhere, counter-stream migrants in sociology texts and White Settlers in the Highlands tend to be noticed for the impact they make on their chosen destinations. But how do they come to exist in the first place? What made an impact on them?

My own experience seems to suggest that the personal evolution which produces a counter-stream migrant can start early in life and may well be linked to the state of the migrant's original community. By 1987, I had long since left the village where I started life, there being nothing either emotional or economic to keep me there. Two big moves later and I was in deepest East Anglia. Here the joke (which I never found very funny but compared with Culloden it's not so bad) was that the locals *would* accept you (suspensory pause) after you'd lived in the village twenty years (another pause) but you'd never be one of them.

In Norfolk, I helped to run a market stall selling secondhand junk. As the older country people died, their heirs flogged off their obsolete left-overs: tin-baths, old bikes with heavy frames and bony saddles, oak-framed pictures of solemn sepia strangers, ginger-beer bottles (collectors' items, you know) biscuit tins (ditto), wind-up gramophones, top-hats, chamber pots and a hundred other newly outlandish objects which had been commonplace until recently. We made a living taking this haul to Cambridge, sixty miles into the future. Here the moderns had ripped everything out of their houses to make room for the display of trophies they got from our stall. We found piles of these desirables at the local auctions in Norfolk. There I met and did deals with the locals. They took my money and kept an eye on my lots for me when I went to get the van at the end of the sale. But I was an outsider. I belonged nowhere and nowhere belonged to me: the perfect qualification for moving all over again.

My decision to come and live in the Highlands of Scotland felt at the time not like a symptom of social deprivation but more like the result of hundreds of frustrations with the steady saturation of English society by Margaret Thatcher's ideas and policies. Even at the start of the 1980s, Scottish society seemed to me, the casual visitor, to be proving comparatively resistant to this virus which appeared intent on destroying so many components of civil society. But all over Britain the damage was being done. Though the changes were shocking at the time, we've grown used to the decimation of the industrial base, to the NHS becoming like a sickly patient who might not make it through another winter. Then, all the Thatcherite works only combined to make me more pessimistic than ever about anything ever occurring which would fill the space, the gap inside my soul where there should have been at least some constructive connection with something like community. Communities themselves were under attack from all directions. I felt drawn to the Highlands as somewhere I might stand a chance of finding and being admitted to a community. Without being at all aware of the contradiction, I also longed for the emptiness of the Highlands which I then believed represented freedom. This illogical combination of desires I now recognise as yet another middle-class, middle-brow, unthought-out escapist urge which when looked at hard appears as nothing so much as the wish to travel back in time to some imaginary better place which had been killed off by the Industrial Revolution. It's easy enough *now* to see the contradictory and illusory qualities of what I was hoping to find when I came north. And if the Iron Lady and all her works supplied the initial inspiration for this half-baked gesture, then the state of the Norfolk countryside did the rest.

A Walk on the Tame Side

East Anglia paunches out over London and is (urban islands apart) like one huge intensive farm with almost every square metre spoken for by profit. Even the uncultivated margins are cut off by fence, shotgun and the law. Many of the fields are so big that you can't see their edges. The whole agribusiness enterprise depends on huge, complicated machinery and millions of pounds worth of chemical fertilisers and weedkillers which, their job done, leach steadily into the water-table. Who can know what long-term effects this will have on plants, animals or people? All I know is that there are days when the tap water there tastes like it has been spiked with a dash of stagnant Domestos.

The so-called unproductive margins, including water meadows and sandy heaths dotted with pine called brecklands, are truly charming but the rest of the prairie-style landscape threatens to overwhelm them. There will be a dust-bowl there: I've often seen quite light winds lifting brown clouds of the earth up and away.

Let me recount a moment or two in the process which led to my departure. I was always searching for bits of countryside which had escaped becoming part of the prairies with their strangely sterile furrows. There was one outstanding remnant of the pre-World War II landscape, a hundred square miles of land kept by the Ministry of Defence for an Army training area since 1945. It was nearly untouched: no sprays, no silage towers and hedges intact, if a little overgrown. The MOD had evacuated several villages whose ruinous remains were now daubed with IRA slogans to remind the boys who the enemy was. This land was called the Battle Area and its perimeters were marked by frequent notices reading, 'MOD – KEEP OUT – Unauthorised Entry is a CRIMINAL OFFENCE.' The serenity of oak, ash and beech posed elegantly behind the signs seemed to mock their fierce declarations. I hung round anyway, drawn to this souvenir of a time before agribusiness, this place of nightingales and badgers. One late winter's afternoon, out of the silence, out of nowhere it seemed, a soldier in full battle dress, blacked-up face and pin-prick pupils, thuds down his black boots on the pathway in front of me. I'm just the wrong side of the fence. He is as perturbed as I am. Does he imagine that I am a part of the exercise he wasn't told about? What should he do with me? I take advantage of his uncertainty to make a speedy return to legality. Once over the fence, I see him mumbling urgently into a walkie-talkie. I do keep out after that: better not push my luck, but that makes one less oasis to escape to from the bleak present. The place remained in my mind, though, as a memorial to what had been destroyed almost completely in the rest of East Anglia.

Another turning point? I was fresh back from yet another trip to the Highlands where I had walked wherever I pleased, eyes opened wide by mountain, moor and sea. I didn't want to stop this gloriously unchecked movement through the landscape. What a silly! Within ten minutes of the radical decision to short-cut across the corner of a ploughed field I was paralysed by great lumps of sticky clay welded to my boots, mocking my attempts to ramble Highlands style, and anyway what would the farmer have said? There were dozens of other dead ends which once I would have grumblingly accepted had it not been for having experienced the miraculous Highlands where only the sea could stop you. Such raptures chose to forget about deer fences.

Once I had decided to come to Scotland, all sorts of people started to give me a hard time about the irresponsibility of my plan. Complaints came under two main headings: I would find earning a living impossible and I wouldn't be able to integrate successfully into the Highland community. Those who accused me of paying insufficient attention to the potential problem areas were quite right. But you know what it's like when you try and tell a friend to be sensible about an affair he or she has embarked on: the smitten hear the words, understand their meanings, but don't have the slightest intention of allowing themselves to be deflected from their chosen course. It was the glorious, mountainous, inspirational landscape which robbed me of common sense. I just had this feeling that if I was able to walk wherever and whenever I liked on those fabulous hills, somehow everything, like work and money, would take care of itself. As for integration: well, didn't the landscape prove that the Highlands was God's country? I equated the absence of people with the presence of God. I comfort myself now with the thought that plenty of post-Industrial Revolution wanna-be nature sprites have made the same mistake. Wordsworth and the 19th century Romantics were guilty of similar delusions and more latterly, conservationists as eminent as John Muir have ignored the human factor when drawing up plans for heaven on earth. It's not very much of a consolation though.

It's only ten years later that I know for sure that the uncultivated emptiness of the Scottish Highlands which made such a delicious change from East Anglia is not an act of God but of man. Every ruin was once a home and many ruins are no longer visible. But the emptiness I relished remains a desolation to many others, the descendants of the evicted and exiled people who once gave this landscape its meaning and vitality. Yet, as I prepared to move my life for the sake of these hills, I was perfectly ignorant of these all-important considerations. I certainly got on well with all the Highlanders I met and was frequently delighted with their anti-authoritarian outlook, but I had never thought of asking them why their land was so empty. For me, it was quite enough that it was empty, marvellously empty: no 'KEEP OUT' signs, no sprays, no barbed wire, only coast-to-coast-to-coast beauty, mine for the walking! And so I arrived, just as the mountain snows were beginning to dwindle, in the spring of 1987. To add the last outrageous touch of irresponsibility, I was pregnant when I made the one-way journey up the A9. I had reassured friends, worried about the problems of integration I might face, with the stunningly naive claim that deciding to have a child in my new country was the ultimate statement of my belief in and commitment to Scotland.

Second Thoughts...

The practical problems involved in making a permanent move to the Highlands had always seemed decisively overwhelming, not least finding a place to rent, an achievement which normally resulted from being well-in with an established social network: impossible, surely, from a distance of over six hundred miles. However, out of the blue, I was offered a two-year lease on a steading (first lesson in Scots: steading = the buildings on a farm, in this case what would have been called a barn in England) which overlooked the Kyle of Sutherland. The steading had been owned along with its neighbouring farmhouse by early vintage White Settlers in the 1960s. Their emigration did not endure but their love affair with the Highlands did and they had kept and converted the steading as a holiday home after selling the sturdy, graceful farmhouse to another incoming English couple: the wave was beginning to build. The two buildings stood alone at the top of a 300 foot hill and apart from another farmhouse and three holiday cottages, the rest of the village sat on the valley bottom. The village was a fair microcosmic representation of the Highlands: English and Scottish incomers (White and Grey Settlers) including a few retired people and some folk (not more than half) who had been born and bred there. The steading was what estate agents might call an imaginative conversion. The huge glass doors at the east end of the L-shaped building had stayed unlocked between holiday visits and had frequently blown open. My first job was to clear the carpet of pine needles which had accumulated on the floor over the winter. My neighbours had been next door for ten years and were welcoming and encouraging without underestimating the problems I was likely to encounter in such an eccentrically appointed house. Both neighbours were actively involved in plenty of local groups: the husband, who had taken early retirement from a distinguished career in the oil industry, was an elder of the local kirk; his wife supported the Scottish Women's Rural Institute, and both were enthusiastic golfers at the local course. They were part of an active community of older people from all over the UK who seemed to have picked the perfect place for a pleasantly busy retirement.

In the first couple of months I didn't have much time or inclination to think too hard about the challenge of the coming winter or about the retired-heavy social composition of my new locale. I was too enchanted by my surroundings and the certain knowledge that, this time, I didn't have to go home to England again: this was home!

It was a truly marvellous spring-time. I gleefully counted all the different wild flowers which flourished along the unsprayed verges. I revelled in the glorious view of field, river, moor and mountain across the Kyle of Sutherland. I gazed spellbound as skeins of greylag geese navigated their northwards passage by the waters of the Kyle. I wrote scores of letters back to England boasting even about the tap water which came neat from a nearby loch. (Europe has since blasphemously done away with its purity by insisting on its chlorination at source.) I fell in love with the sound and idiom of the Highland voice though it was difficult to follow at first. I even wrote a piece for the wafer-thin local paper, *The Northern Times*. In it I listed all the reasons why I was so delighted to have come to the Highlands. God knows what they made of it in Brora: just another English wifie paid by the deeply conservative raggie to patronise the locals? I wanted to sign the piece *White Settler*; this idea was politely but firmly rejected by the editor. He was well aware that such irony might well miss its mark completely.

Yet by midsummer this golden time of careless rapture was nearly over. Tiny doubts about the rightness of my being in Scotland at all started whispering in my ear and they wouldn't go away. Perhaps these doubts began with an unexpectedly powerful sense of how foreign a country Scotland is. All those comfortable similarities to England, with language at the top of the list, suddenly seemed superficial in comparison with the many concrete differences between the two countries.

My first surprise was the discovery that Scotland had a culture of its own which had little to do with the kitsch stereotypes of tartan tight-fistedness so readily and thoughtlessly accepted in England. This culture also seemed far more vibrant at a grass-roots level than any equivalent in England. In the Highlands, at any rate, distance from the big urban centres seemed to inspire, not inhibit, cultural activity. Among the numerous examples of this which I spotted in the local paper were piping recitals, local history groups, tuition for, and performance of, traditional dance and music, clan associations, amateur dramatic and choral performances, artists' and writers' groups and widespread and varied religious observance. Most strikingly, participation as far as I could see did not seem to be restricted to the middle-classes. Of course, not everyone took part, but those who did seemed to form a good socio-economic cross-section of the whole population.

BBC Radio Scotland was another exciting discovery. Most of its programmes displayed a marked degree of Scottish historical and cultural self-awareness and presumed an intelligent audience with an informed interest and pride in Scotland. Yet despite its excellent entertainment and information value, Radio Scotland helped all sorts of my vague doubts to crystallise. To begin with, programmes like folk singer Jimmy MacGregor's *Gathering* kept reminding me that unlike all its guests and seemingly most of the audience, I knew nothing of Scottish history, geography, politics, literature or traditions. I was fascinated by the regular local history features but was completely unable to understand them in a greater historical framework. I realised that at school and university where I had studied European, African and Indian history, the history of England's closest neighbour was only ever studied as and when it impinged on English affairs. Scotland was given no attention in its own right, but only looked at through English-coloured spectacles. A more depressing effect of regular listening to *Radio Scotland* was the discovery that generally the English were not thought of very highly by the articulate and interesting Scots appearing on the network. Not many words were spent on expressing these negative feelings but one could sense their existence. It seemed to be tacitly understood and agreed that somehow the English, as a nation, if not as individuals, were generally in the wrong.

Then came politics to confirm the wisdom of this anti-English bias. About six weeks after I arrived in the Highlands, Margaret Thatcher won her third General Election victory. The Tories were in absolute charge of the UK with only a handful of seats in Scotland. It dawned on me what this meant: the Scottish Secretary of State was a sort of unelected King of Scotland governing through a squad of quangos with no majority of popular support. I was hard put to decide what shocked me most: that such unfairness should exist in a so-called mature democracy or that I had never had the slightest inkling before that this was the incredible case and I thought I knew a fair bit about British politics and history. So, it seemed like a long list of bad news had originated '*down the road*' (Highland-speak for from the south) and that we White Settlers in our increasing numbers were just another dose of it.

As well as the General Election result, 1987 also saw a significant gap emerge between property prices in the south and north of Britain. A short-lived, and for many, ultimately disastrous boom in house prices in the south of England enabled an influx of English to make a move north to significantly more substantial properties than they'd left behind. I had only moved from one rented property to another but I still felt uncomfortable when the wits on *Radio Scotland* did their jokes about English incomers swapping outside privvies in Hackney for Highland estates.

The 1987 house price boom was possibly the last time the sun shone full-beam on Mrs Thatcher's England. Its collapse, the fiasco of the poll tax in 1988 and the apparent demise of

Communism in 1989 combined to take the shine off the Iron Lady. But in 1987 she was looking invincible in a way which was particularly offensive to many people in Scotland. I found myself in a situation which ironical was too mild a word to describe. I had come to Scotland to escape from the enchantment with which Margaret Thatcher had apparently ensnared most of England, and yet as a potentially unpopular Englishwoman suddenly I felt we had a lot in common, Maggie and me... and that really did make me feel uncomfortable.

I was excited to be asked to a Midsummer Solstice bonfire party thinking this would be an important step on the path to an exciting, integrated social life. By midgy midnight I was ready for home. Wild men in kilts and grimy t-shirts – whom I never met again – jumped, roaring, over the Beltane bonfire and polished off a lot of cheap whisky. I sat weighed down and silenced with an unavoidable sense of them and me growing stronger by the minute and for the first time, while busy trying to look as if I belonged, was addressed wryly, rather than rudely, as White Settler.

Indeed after just a few weeks I had become uncomfortably aware of the preponderance of English people in the Highlands. They truly were everywhere: shops and offices, castles and council houses, antique shops and car boot sales, on the local radio station and in dole queues. I only had to look at the small area where I had landed. In the villages which contained most of the local population there was a Church of Scotland minister from England, two English doctors, a couple of shopkeepers from England and a phalanx of worthy English retireds who seemed to dominate many of the local clubs and committees, the pipe band being a notable exception. Even the wife of the nationally famous but locally born Highland Seer came from Stockport. Sitting by that bonfire and many times in subsequent weeks I wondered if the size of the English presence did not constitute an imbalance which threatened the survival of the very social world which the incomers had chosen to inhabit. There were so many more English in the Highlands than I had ever expected. Instead of being part of a daring minority I felt more like one of an outsize gang of gate-crashers who, through their inappropriate arrival, have brought to an end the very party they wanted to join.

The summer moved on. By the time the parade of wild flowers was passed and I'd heard the stags bellowing sex and territory for the first unforgettable time, I knew two things for sure. First, life in the Highlands was going to be more complicated than I'd ever imagined. Second, however complicated things might be, I'd tasted the undeniable sweetness of life in the north: the endlessly enchanting landscape and the pure air and water. The idea of going back to England was unbearable. So, as I braced myself for my first winter, I knew what I had to do.

More and more, I realised that the historical relationship between the English and Scots and their two countries needed careful examination. There was my personal sense of being a stranger in a strange land, suddenly culturally illiterate: what is a pibroch, where is Strathspey, why is a Mod, who is a kilt, when is yestreen? There were bits of basic Scottish history and geography about which I was hopelessly ignorant. When you grow up in a country, you absorb and experience information about it as you go along. So, in a new country you are automatically bereft of familiarity with how and why things got to be the way they are. This is especially true for the English in Scotland: it seems like home until you arrive and find that it isn't. These two old countries, Scotland and England, are apparently close enough to be thought of as family by the rest of the world. I wonder if the English exodus to Scotland has been inspired by the idea of that country as the place of some favourite, if occasionally cantankerous, relative where the English know they will be able to enjoy thrillingly different vistas and experiences but where they will also be made to feel safe in the way family makes you feel safe with recognisable things: stamps, road signs, telephone boxes, pints of bitter and the BBC, for example. However, at certain crucial moments the cosy familiarity is impossible to maintain. Such moments include international football tournaments, trial imposition of new taxes, midnight on any 31st December and the day after yet another General Election result has rubbed Scotland's face in its inability to achieve proper democratic self-expression. I turned to history for at least the possibility of enlightenment.

Why Fort William, Fort Augustus, Fort George? Military occupation? But I thought we were a family! A little bit of history explains the post-1745 rationale for it – but what does history make of an army of occupation that never left? At any time there may be up to 600 soldiers stationed at Fort George overlooking the Moray Firth. How were Highlanders transformed from threatening savages into perfectly betartaned residents of these pristine buildings just a hop from Drumossie Muir where the Young Pretender's campaign came to its bloody and inglorious end? I needed to know and understand more history than could be written on a tin of shortbread.

Events in the present conspired to make me determined to do my best to disentangle some of these contradictions and incongruities. The first big one came in June 1987, six weeks after I became a full-time Highland resident. This would have been about the time when I was fiercely replying to the common question, 'Where do you stay?' with 'Oh, I'm not staying anywhere: I live here.' Then I experienced, along with the rest of Scotland, the bizarre workings of what I had always, from South of the border, been happy to think of as a functioning UK-wide democracy. The only response I could muster was a sense of trouble stored up, of wrong done, unfairness institutionalised and justified.

The unacceptability of the 1987 election result was clear.
Scotland did count for something as a country to the Scots themselves if not the English. After only this short time it was obvious to
me that more Scots felt something for their country and its national
traditions than most English people did about theirs. I have already
described how I had noticed evidence for this across the social
spectrum in those first weeks including pipe bands, Gaelic classes,
kilts everywhere, the Kirk and Radio Scotland which broadcast
excellent programmes devoted, in a totally accessible way, to Scots
history and culture. This impression was strengthened by
comparison with England. There, patriotism, like many other
national institutions, is shaped largely by the class system. It isn't
totally a preserve of the well-to-do, but it nearly is. Intellectuals
enjoy the luxury of cosmopolitanism thanks to the long-established
security of English nationhood and the relative ease of foreign
travel. They also are often a little embarrassed about the Empire.
Scotland, the country with the most clearly visible sense of national
identity, was the one to suffer from enforced political inarticulacy.

Then, as if to prove the immediate reality of the electoral
iniquities of June, I started to hear a lot about Fountain Forestry.
The Conservative Government had passed a law which must have
sounded great in England: tax breaks for the super-rich if they
invested in tree-planting. Green? Yes, but the wrong shade.
Fountain Forestry made a fortune by doing the planting of these
tax break acres. They planted hundreds of thousands of acres of
non-native conifers in sterile, unnatural rows which made a dreary
desert of trees. Eventually it would be just possible to make toilet
paper out of them. I watched anxiously for the first signs of
plantations: the furrows, ready for the seedlings, gouged out of
black peat and white stone, snaking round the contour of the hills.
I also saw the other end of the process: the devastation left after
conifer plantations were felled. It reminded me of photographs of
the wreckage of the French countryside after World War I.

By the autumn of my first year in the Highlands I had begun to feel distinctly uneasy. There was snow on the hills by the middle of October and I wondered if the woodburner would be equal to the winter when it arrived down at the steading. Just after I spotted the snow, I spent a week in Raigmore Hospital after my daughter was born. The colours I saw on my journey back to Sutherland were absolutely gorgeous: the rich dark green of gorse and heather, the dull copper of old bracken, the plum clouds of the bare birch trees and intense aquamarine of the Kyle of Sutherland where the swans looked like pearls studded on dark velvet. October colours in Norfolk? Different shades of mud and black, bare branches reaching from the flat earth into the huge skies. How could I go back?

So, I was staying and was delighted to be called on by my neighbours wishing the baby well. I received one pair of visitors, though, who didn't delight me. Rather, they whipped up all the uncertainties and doubts I had about being in the Highlands. These must have been nudged out of focus during the momentous events in the hospital and the kindness and warmth with which I had been looked after there and which greeted my return.

Ken and Rosemary were perfectly pleasant and had come round to say welcome to the neighbourhood and to see the new baby. Originally from Essex, they had been living in the Highlands for seven years and had bought a house twenty miles inland from my steading. We sat round the woodburner and drank tea and they told me all about their life. They rattled on cheerfully, friendly to each other and to me as they divulged all sorts of local information and gossip which they thought I would find helpful and interesting.

But their visit provided me with a reflection of myself I did not enjoy recognising. Their reasons for moving to the Highlands had been very similar to mine: clean and beautiful landscape plus peace and quiet. And from what they had to say it seemed that plenty of other English people had had roughly the same idea. Ken and Rosemary told me all about the numerous English incomers to the district, where they lived and the various ways they earned their livings. This roll-call of craft-workers (Ken and Rosemary had a glass engraving business), artists, agricultural handymen and would-be crofters made my heart sink. It seemed as if there were millions of English here already which didn't do much for the image I had had of myself as intrepid, lone pioneer, a vision already dented by the presence of so many retired English in the area. Now Rosemary and Ken were completely finishing it off. What a thought: scores of English people charging north up the A9 on the hunt for peace and quiet only to discover when they arrive scores of English people on the hunt for – peace and quiet.

Then there was the way my visitors spoke. Don't misunderstand me: I'm not an accent snob. I admit that Essex is not my favourite vocal flavour, but it wasn't their accent which disturbed me. What I had never heard before that evening was ordinary English voices casually trotting out words and phrases which I firmly felt belonged to the Scots. It was my visitors' use of och and aye that mainly caught my ear and I supposed this *Scoto voce* must have been picked up during their years of living and working with Scots. I wasn't just disturbed by this linguistic incongruity but also jealous of the couple's apparently successful integration into the local life and economy. Under the heading of interesting and useful information they told me about all the different jobs they had done since coming north: forestry, farm-work and fish-farming all over the Highlands. My only serious attempts to earn money since my arrival had been linked to England where I had been sending articles about my wonderful new home and now it looked as though I'd be spending the winter on the dole. That didn't feel much like the act of a brave pioneer either. I knew it was silly to be upset by my visitors having made more useful connections in seven years that I had in a few months. But I couldn't get used to their use of Scottish words. Their ochs and ayes seemed unselfconscious but it sounded somehow wrong if not intentionally phoney to me. Or was I just envious of their at-homeness? Before they left, I asked them if they knew anything about the Battle of Carbisdale which had occurred in 1651 on the very hillside where my steading was. My next-door neighbours had told me that much. I found a further account in a child's history book I had brought from England. The fifth Earl of Montrose, who had lost the battle, had escaped across country to Ardvreck Castle on the shores of Loch Assynt some thirty miles to the west. The story of Montrose's betrayal to his enemies by his Macleod host there and his subsequent execution in Edinburgh fascinated me for I had seen Ardvreck Castle. Its gaunt ruins testify to the power of the curse which fell on Macleod for breaking the sacrosanct laws of Highland hospitality. But I wanted some proper historical context for all this fairy tale stuff. What had Montrose given his life for? Who had ordered his execution and why? I wanted goodies and baddies or a least a full *dramatis personae*. But Ken and Rosemary had never heard of the battle or Montrose and didn't seem at all interested in the history of the Highlands. That was odder to me than their ochs and ayes.

Someone had given me a coffee-table history of Scotland as a going-away present. I found a reference to Carbisdale which included a contemporary picture of Montrose (a bit of a pin-up I thought but then felt a bit peculiar when I went on to read that after being hanged and then disembowelled his corpse had been pinned up for a year as a warning to other traitors). The section concluded with the verses engraved on his tombstone when his remains were given a proper burial at St Giles, Edinburgh in 1888.

Scotland's glory, Britain's pride,
As brave a subject as ere for his monarch dy'd.
Kingdoms in ruins often lye
But great Montrose's Acts will never dye.

Why had Montrose been executed if he'd been so loyal to his monarch? And what was this Covenant with which he seemed to have had a fair amount to do. One thing was clear: Scotland in 1650 was still very much a separate country with its own history. This history could never be properly understood if it were only seen as noises off from the main attraction of English events and agenda.

There was another thing: the writer of the verse prophecy had never imagined: the advent to the Highlands of hundreds of outsiders most of whom had not forgotten Montrose but had probably never heard of him. Moreover, these people had come freely from a country with whom Scotland was joined in a Union which had claimed since its inception to be fair and equal to both the partners. Now, in 1988, events seemed to be piling up which showed the Union to be the very reverse of such an equitable arrangement.

That year, the Conservatives presented the whole Scottish electorate with a more concrete reminder of the political power they had won in the previous year. The political background to the Community Charge is described in some detail later in this book. For now, suffice to say, it was a dreadful way for me to mark the end of my first year in Scotland. The Poll Tax confirmed unmistakeably the uncomfortable realisations which had been growing since my arrival the previous spring-time. The whole scheme seemed inherently wrong-headed but its introduction in Scotland a year ahead of the rest of the UK seemed absolutely to flaunt the arbitrary unfairness of the Union. How could the Westminster government be allowed to behave so, within a democracy? And why did this feel so familiar, just another bitter helping of traditional south/north discourse? My sense of trouble stored up increased.

After the 1987 election and the Poll Tax, a definite sense existed of grass-roots Scots determination to change the constitutional arrangements which were producing such undesirable and unfair outcomes. The Constitutional Convention which had representation from at first all anti-Unionist parties then all minus the SNP, was the marker of this new mood. This mood was scunnered by the General Election result of 1992 but not defeated by it.

There were some who were inclined to comment at the same time on the ever-growing numbers of English who were settling in Scotland. Groups like Scottish Watch and Settler Watch appeared, dotted all around Scotland, spray-painting their uncompromising opposition to English incomers who they claimed were taking Scots' jobs and houses. One of their spokesmen, Patrick White, a publican from Inverness, banned English people from his pub. Fortunately for everyone in Scotland these groups did not turn out to be the beginnings of anything very much. In the Highlands at any rate, the anti-racist backlash was sufficiently vigorous to put an end to these groups' campaigning openly.

Yet, all in all, by 1993, despite looking locally, nationally and globally I couldn't find much help in solving the puzzle I had chosen for myself by coming to Scotland. I wanted to avoid blaming the English and feeling guilty or blaming the Scots and feeling angry. Yet I could not avoid a sense that deep-seated historical iniquities were exerting a powerful influence on the present. I gradually determined that as well as avoiding fault-finding, I must refuse to be part of any process which kept the fault alive. How was that to be done?

It seemed that, although nearly a decade had passed since I stopped being a history student, some systematic history was what

I needed to do. It might be some help in filling in the gaps of my day-to-day understanding of my new home and, more importantly, it might explain some of the puzzles in the relationship between England and Scotland. As I now found myself very much on the problematic frontier of this relationship, history, however daunting, looked like it might provide some of the answers.

CHAPTER 3

A Brief History of the Scots and the English

Unequal Geographies

" Who are you that so strangely woke,
  And raised a fine hand?"
Poverty wears a scarlet cloke
           In my land.

" Duchies of dreamland, emerald, rose
  Lie at your command?"
Poverty like a princess goes
           In my land.

The Princess of Scotland, Rachel Annand Taylor

FROM THIS DISTANCE TWO aspects of the pre-historical situation are crucial. First is the basic geographical comparison between the two areas we now call Scotland and England: Scotland comprises one third the area of the island where the two countries are situated. Of Scotland's total land area three-fifths is mountain, hill or moor and one-fifth is classified as rough grazing or grass. This leaves only one-fifth of the total area which is productively fertile. The fraction of England unsuitable for cultivation is, at the most, one-fifth which makes England significantly the stronger of the two in terms of pre-industrial economic potential. Another disadvantageous aspect of Scotland's geography is the difficulty of establishing communications and hence central political authority over mountainous terrain and around a sharply-indented coastline.

So we see, from the very beginning, the scales are tipped against Scotland in its relationship with England. What it most puts me in mind of is two young brothers who, because of their physical proximity, are bound to fight. The smaller one will never be able to beat the bigger one but neither is the match so uneven that he won't ever attempt it. The bigger one doesn't get it all his own way. The wild, tortuous terrain of Scotland is dominated by Druim Alban which is a spine-like ridge of high mountains. These stretch from Ben Lomond in Central Scotland to Ben Hope on the north coast and meant that until 1746, when the single-mindedness of Hanoverian plans to police the whole of Scotland led to a road and bridge building programme, the complete control of Scotland by an invading power was impossible.

The other important fact we can grasp from historical conjecture is one which makes a nonsense of any suggestion that a discussion about Scots and English as separate races rests on sound ethnic foundations. The facts, as far as they are agreed, are of absolutely no use to anybody who is out trying to make a case for the Scots and the English being inherently different. The four regions which became the component parts of Great Britain were, after the retreat of the ice-sheet and the submerging of the land bridge to Europe (c.6000-5000BC), colonised by the same mix of peoples. The original Scots came from Ireland and settled on the west coast. To the west also and to the south came people from the Mediterranean, c.2000BC. Their journey had taken them *via* Cornwall and Wales where they also settled. Later, c.1800BC, migrations to the east coast of the whole island were made from Holland and the Rhineland. Some of the next wave of arrivals, c.1600BC, also came from the European mainland *via* England. It is not within the scope of this book to go into serious archaeological analysis of these earliest inhabitants of what would later be called Scotland. Suffice to say that megalithic monuments, bronze and iron age burial practices and surviving artefacts from across England, Scotland, Wales and Ireland show that the original inhabitants of these territories came from the same selection of places. Just as there is no such thing as a purely Scottish or English person, neither is there a pedigree which is the sole property of either modern nation.

The first point where conjecture is replaced by an understanding based on at least a few facts is Roman Britain. By this time Scotland was peopled with tribes which had emerged from the successive waves of arrivals over the previous two thousand years. Gnaeus Julius Agricola, Roman governor of Britain (77-84AD) was the first Roman to operate extensively in Scotland. Roman historians claimed that he defeated some of these tribes at the Battle of Mons Graupius (probably fought somewhere in Banffshire) in 84AD. However, the Roman Empire could not spare troops for his goal of containing the war-like tribes of the Highland zone. Subsequent Roman policy concentrated on establishing a viable frontier, first by building the Antonine Wall, a turf and stone structure between the Firth and Clyde. Ultimately, further south, Hadrian built over seventy miles of fortified stone wall to be the permanent northern frontier of Roman Britain. After Agricola, the Romans never had the capacity to subjugate the whole of Scotland. Their legacy was most enduring in the south of Britain which they had according to their own fashion civilised. There are no Roman village remains to be found further north than the Vale of York. Scotland, however, was never civilised nor occupied. The Roman influence which had such a marked effect on English law, customs and civic development was practically unknown in Scotland apart from the small-scale trading which took place in the area of Hadrian's Wall. This is the first instance of the north and south parts of these islands having markedly different historical experiences.

The Establishment of the Scottish Monarchy

Where we are, there's daggers in men's smiles: the near in blood,
The nearer bloody.

Macbeth, William Shakespeare

The next four hundred years are scantily chronicled. However, by 800AD four distinct tribes had emerged in Scotland: the teutonic-speaking Angles, the Scots from northern Ireland, the Britons centred in the south-west and the Picts who occupied Scotland north of the Forth. The 8th century saw a new force invading from the north, the Vikings whose land-hungry expeditions round the whole coast of Scotland helped to create the formation of a unified territory. The marauding presence of Viking longships tended to isolate the northern territory of the British Isles and gave its various tribes a compelling reason to unite.

In 843, Kenneth MacAlpin, King of Scots, also became King of the Picts. Helped in part by the Norse threat, he was able to establish the new kingdom of Alba in which the Scots' pre-eminence probably reflects a tendency established before 843. The danger posed by the Norse invaders also prompted the first official alliance between the territories which would become England and Scotland. In exchange for help on land and sea (against the Vikings), Edmund of England leased Cumbria to Malcolm I of Scotland. It would be nearly a thousand years before the two countries were similarly threatened by a common foe from across the water and over seven hundred years before the last military conflict between England and Scotland took place on the disputed border at the Battle of Pinkie, 1547.

Malcolm I, who died in battle against the men of Moray in 954, was a great-grandson of Kenneth MacAlpin. The succession had come down in a way which marks the Celtic character of the early

Scottish monarchy. This type of succession is called tanistry and meant a king could be succeeded by any male member of a group drawn from collateral branches of his family. It led to many instances of a king succeeding to the throne by killing his predecessor. For example, Duncan I was killed by his cousin, Macbeth, in 1040 and Macbeth was killed by Duncan's son, Malcolm III Canmore, in 1057. However, Malcolm III Canmore has been described as the last of the Celtic kings. The replacement of tanistry by primogeniture and the growing importance of non-Celtic language mark the development most clearly. Malcolm III Canmore (c.1031-1093) stands on the boundary of this change. His first wife, Ingeborg, was the daughter of a Norse Earl of Orkney but after her death his second marriage marked his recognition of the importance of his southern neighbour. In 1069, he married Margaret, sister of Edgar Atheling, heir to the Saxon throne which had been seized by William of Normandy.

Malcolm adored his English wife, allowing her to introduce many English customs to the court, and acquiescing in her plans for religious reform. Her refusal to learn Gaelic symbolised her opposition to the existing traditions of the Scottish monarchy. Her presence at Malcolm's side also set the bloody ball of Anglo-Scottish conflict rolling for the next five hundred years when William of Normandy noticed that Malcolm Canmore's court had become a haven for fleeing Saxons. Initially, Malcolm offered fealty to William but soon resumed his attempts to extend the Scottish kingdom southwards. Malcolm and his son, Edward, died fighting the Normans at Alnwick in 1093.

For the next century, Scottish government was dominated by a conflict between the families of Malcolm Canmore's two wives. Ingeborg's descendants opposed the introduction of primogeniture and other Anglo-Norman customs which had been adopted by Margaret's descendants as they sought to strengthen their own position and to increase the strength of Scotland by introducing more effective government on Anglo-Norman feudal lines. Not only did they personally make important marriage alliances with the English ruling class but they also offered land to many Norman magnates in order to gain their assistance in establishing an effective feudal monarchy and in putting an end to the Celtic aspirations of Ingeborg's descendants.

David I, who reigned from 1124-1153, was pre-eminent in carrying out this policy of feudalisation. The Anglo-Norman arrivals during his reign included the Bruces, the De Morvilles and the Fitzalans, who later became the Stewarts.

The next one hundred and fifty years saw the Scottish monarchy

Malcolm IV	1153 – 1165
William I	1165 – 1214
Alexander II	1214 – 1249
Alexander III	1249 – 1289

consolidating its territorial control, establishing a degree of commercial growth and fending off English claims of feudal superiority without recourse to warfare.

The Wars of Independence

For so long as but one hundred of us remain alive, we will yield in no least way to English dominion. For we fight not for glory nor for riches nor for honour but only and alone for freedom, which no good man surrenders but with his life.

The Declaration of Arbroath, 1320

In 1286, primogeniture and feudalism, Scotland's most important Anglo-Norman imports combined to open a second bloodier act in the conflict between Scotland and England. Alexander III and his primogenitive heir, his young grand-daughter, Margaret, Maid of Norway, died within four years of each other leaving the succession to the Scottish throne uncertain.

Edward I's son had been betrothed to the Maid in an arrangement which treated England and Scotland equally as sovereign parties. However, after her death Edward pressed his claims of feudal superiority over Scotland and demanded the right to adjudicate between the rival claimants to the Scottish throne. When his choice of successor to the Maid, John Balliol, refused to do military service for him in France and concluded an alliance with that country instead, Edward marched north, sacked Berwick, massacred its inhabitants and proceeded to force Scotland's complete submission. A highly symbolic measure of this extreme humiliation was enacted during Edward's triumphal progress through Scotland. From Scone he took the Coronation Stone on which ancient Scottish Kings were enthroned and from Edinburgh he took the Black Rood of St Margaret. Despite an attempt to rescue it in the 1950s, the Stone of Scone was kept at Westminster Abbey until 1996. Given John Major's refusal to countenance any constitutional reform of the Union, his decision to return the Stone never appeared more than a meaningless gesture.

However, there was already a sophisticated sense of national unity in 13th century Scotland as evidenced by the resistance of the Community of Realm (important laymen and church leaders) to Edward's tactless, then oppressive insistence on his feudal rights over Scotland.

William Wallace, second son of a Renfrewshire knight, took the initiative against Edward and won a dazzling victory against the English at Stirling Bridge in 1297. He was defeated at Falkirk the following year and subjected to an agonising death in London in 1305 as a punishment for treason against a king to whom he had never sworn loyalty. Edward set up an administration in Scotland and was able to weaken the threat of noble revolt by buying the support of magistrates. Robert Bruce, whose grandfather had been one of the Competitors for the succession to the Maid of Norway, rose in revolt against Edward's government in 1306, thereby supplying an effective focus for the growing movement of national resistance. Edward's death in 1307 and the weakness of English resolve under Edward II played into Robert's hands. He won a crucial battle against Edward II at Bannockburn on Midsummer's Day, 1314. The military victory was complete, bringing substantial booty from the defeated English forces. Most importantly, it secured Scottish independence and established Bruce as King Robert I of Scotland. This was confirmed by a Scottish Parliament in the November of the same year. However, the tendency of the Scots nobles to put their own interests before loyalty to an independent Scottish kingdom was already sufficiently strong to make it a priority for Bruce to ensure their loyalty. The Declaration of Arbroath is best remembered for its quintessentially Scots expression of the importance of freedom: 'For we fight not for glory nor for riches nor for honour but only and alone for freedom, which no good man surrenders but with his life.' The Declaration was also a clever piece of politics for it committed its noble signatories to continued support for Scottish independence against threats and bribes from England. Robert's last great achievement was the Treaty of Northampton (1328) by which England recognised Scotland's independence.

In 1329, Bruce died and his son, David II succeeded to the throne, aged five. In 1332 Edward Balliol, son of John, Edward I's choice of successor to the Maid of Norway, invaded Scotland on the pretext of recovering his rightful throne. Supported by Edward III, he gained the allegiance of disaffected Scots nobles. Some of these had suffered forfeiture of their lands through being on the English side at Bannockburn. Some of them, in a tradition which lasted well beyond the Wars of Independence, simply saw the vulnerability of the Scottish king as a chance to further their own interests: the inevitable result of the proximity of England as an alternative source of power. David lost the battle of Halidon Hill near Berwick to the combined forces of John Balliol and Edward III and in 1334 had to flee to France – a regular haven for Scottish kings because of the enmity between France and England. He returned in 1341 but was captured by the English at the Battle of Neville's Cross, near Durham. He was released in 1357 in exchange for a huge ransom which, like the rest of the high cost of the Wars of Independence, had the effect of significantly retarding Scotland's economic and hence social development.

The Early Stewarts

Any man who refuses to help the King against his rebels shall himself be accounted a rebel.

Enactment from James I's first Parliament, 1424

David was succeeded by the first of the Stewart Kings, Robert II, a son of Robert Bruce's daughter, Marjorie and Walter Stewart. Readers, especially those who tire of historical detail, will be relieved to learn we can summarise the early Stewart kings

Robert II	1371 – 1390
Robert III	1390 – 1406
James I	1406 – 1437
James II	1437 – 1460
James III	1460 – 1488

as being beset by a recurring set of disadvantages which accounted for the monarchical weakness of most of this period.

Primogeniture proved disastrous for Scotland. James I, II and III succeeded as minors, a fact which exacerbated the tendency of the nobles to put their own interests before those of the monarch. The Douglases and the Lords of the Isles seriously threatened royal authority in this way. James I was murdered by noble conspirators who planned to seize the throne for Walter Stewart. James II was only six when he became king but he grew up determined to strengthen the position of the monarchy and sought successfully to end the power of the Douglas family. He was killed at the Siege of Roxburgh which had recovered one of the last Scottish territories still in English hands. His son, James III, succeeded at the age of eight. The continuous threat of noble intrigue and its encouragement by England is evidenced in the Treaty of Westminster – Ardtornish (1462). Edward IV used the exiled Black Douglas to negotiate with John, Lord of the Isles. The treaty bound John to become liegeman of the King of England and to work with Douglas to carve Scotland into two vassal states of England led by themselves. This alliance came to nothing but Berwick fell once more to the English in 1482, largely due to reluctance of the nobles, led by Archibald Douglas, to support their king against the English. James III was murdered, like his grandfather, after a battle against his noble opponents at Sauchieburn, but his son, James IV, succeeded without difficulty. Within two years he had rid himself of the baronial faction which had opposed his father. An able, cultured and popular king, he encountered little opposition from the nobles. He was, for example, able to achieve the forfeiture of the Lords of the Isles in 1493, thereby doing much to ensure Scottish territorial integrity against threats to it by English diplomacy. A power vacuum was thus created on the western coast, however, of which English influence was later able to take decisive advantage.

Throughout the Wars of Independence England's frequent wars with France made the Auld Alliance an obvious strategic choice for

Scotland. Trading links were strong between the two countries. Robert the Bruce had made the Treaty of Corbeil with France in 1326 under which neither Scotland nor France could make peace with England if the other was at war with her. Subsequent Scottish kings saw France as a haven from English threats or hostile noble factions. James IV renewed the Auld Alliance in 1513 to counterbalance the anti-French Alliance between England and the Papacy. In 1513 Henry VIII invaded France and James IV consequently and rashly invaded England. The disastrous Battle of Flodden in which James, with a generation of Scotland's leading men, lost his life ended an episode of promising monarchical energy and strength. James IV's reign is notable for a powerful flourishing of Scots literature from the makars, Robert Henryson and William Dunbar among others. Of critical consequence to Scotland's history was James's marriage in 1503 to Henry VII's daughter, Margaret. This linked the Royal Houses of Scotland and England inextricably.

Rough Wooing

[I] did not so much mislike the [English] match as the rough manner of wooing.

Earl of Huntly, 1547

In 1513, James V succeeded his father at the age of two. During his minority the nobility was divided over the benefits of continuing the alliance with France. When James came of age he chose France and concluded two marriages with the French ruling house. His second wife, Mary de Guise, became the mother of Mary, Queen of Scots. James's pro-French policy and his vigorous fiscal regime deprived him of the nobility's wholehearted support. This fact was more than likely to blame for his defeat by the English at Solway Moss in November, 1542. Henry VIII had embarked on his break from

Rome and wanted to force Scotland to follow his line rather than pursue its alliance with Catholic France. Many of the Scots nobles, once their own country's Reformation was underway, had similar religious objections to the French alliance. James died within a month of Solway Moss. His one surviving child, Mary, was just one week old. As a half-French Catholic princess with a Tudor grand-mother, her tragic fate seems almost inevitable given the rising tide of the Scottish Reformation and the global intensification of religious conflict. As had happened in England, a mixture of a general search for spiritual renewal and the nobles' desire to appropriate church lands made Scotland very receptive to the message of religious reform coming from Germany. However, Henry VIII's heavy-handed policies for dominating Scotland had caused Scots' hatred of the Auld Enemy to intensify. Henry asserted his power over Scotland in a way reminiscent of Edward I, insisting on custody of Mary and a promise of the Scottish throne in the event of her death. Such overbearing demands produced an inevitable reaction.

At the start of Mary's minority a pro-French faction seized control. Mary's proposed marriage to Edward, the Tudor heir, was cancelled in favour of a union with the French Dauphin. Mary set sail to be Queen of France in 1548 leaving as Regent her mother, Mary of Guise. France helped Scotland to defeat the angered English but inevitably Scots opposition grew to this French Catholic domination. The gathering momentum of the Scottish Reformation and the death of Mary of Guise in 1560 led to calls for Scotland's rejection of France in favour of England and a peace treaty was signed between Scotland and England in 1560. England appeared to be fostering the Scottish Reformation but was chiefly concerned with the danger of French influence at the court of Mary, a strong claimant to the English succession. Mary's Tudor blood derived from impeccable sources, unlike that of Henry's successor,

Elizabeth, whose mother, Anne Boleyn, had married Henry after his divorce from Katherine of Aragon. This meant the marriage was, by 16th century standards, of questionable validity. John Knox, the powerful inspiration of the by now well-established Scottish Reformation, described the arrival of the Catholic queen as bringing Scotland 'sorrow, dolour, darkness and all impiety'.

However, most of the sorrow caused by her return to Scotland she experienced herself. There is no evidence that she intended to reverse the Reformation in Scotland, being content to celebrate Mass privately at Holyrood. She was prepared to co-operate with the Reformed Church in financial matters. But religious schism now dominated European politics. Mary's second marriage could have had immense strategic importance if, for a likely example, she married into one of the Catholic Royal Houses. Mary's claim to the English throne meant her marriage represented an extreme threat to Elizabeth's security. In 1565 she married Darnley, son of the Earl of Lennox. He was a Catholic, so Knox and the nobles who lost control of Mary to Darnley and his family were opposed to the marriage. Their armed protest came to nothing, however. Darnley, though, did not fulfil Mary's expectations and she was forced to exclude him from her counsels. He turned to the Protestant nobility and convinced them to murder Mary's secretary, Riccio, as a papal spy. This was done by Darnley and others in Mary's private rooms. The nobles then seized power but Mary escaped to the Dunbar castle of the Earl of Bothwell. Knox and the Protestant nobles behind the murder fled as Mary returned to Edinburgh in triumph. The next year Darnley died in suspicious circumstances and shortly afterwards the Earl of Bothwell's 'abduction' of Mary ended in their marriage. Bothwell had only recently been divorced for adultery. The strange death of her second husband and the unsuitability of her third lost Mary significant support in Scotland. She was seized by nobles claiming to be rescuing her from Bothwell. She was imprisoned and, in July 1567, her son, James VI, aged thirteen months, was crowned King of Scotland. The following year Mary escaped to England hoping (unwisely for the strategic reasons already mentioned) for Elizabeth's help. The Protestant supporter of Elizabeth, the Earl of Moray was now Regent in Scotland and Elizabeth was unlikely to help Mary against him. The European Wars of Religion continued; the Pope had excommunicated Elizabeth. She could not afford to be anything less than certain of a neutral northern frontier. Mary's fate was, therefore, decided. After sixteen years of imprisonment by Elizabeth, she was executed for treason after Walsingham's Secret Service had uncovered an inept plot to free Mary and assassinate Elizabeth.

Mary's personal tragedy derived from the immense danger she represented to Queen Elizabeth. Like many Scottish monarchs before her, she was tyrannised by England. She suffered these extreme consequences because she represented a religious, strategic and dynastic threat to the Protestant succession in England. Her fate is a particularly striking example of England's refusal to tolerate any threat from her northern neighbour.

Possibly James VI's strongest feeling about his mother, Mary, detained far away in England for nearly all his life was anxiety lest she should somehow interfere with his succession to the English throne. Elizabeth had supported James Douglas, fourth Earl of Morton, during James's minority, but she would not commit herself to guaranteeing James's succession to her own throne. It is possible that James's attempts to secure the survival of Episcopacy in the Scottish church had been undertaken with an eye to pleasing Elizabeth who violently disapproved of the Puritanism which had gained strong support in Scotland. James was also reluctant to pursue Catholic noble plotters and he maintained diplomatic links with Catholic Europe. Yet his eye never left the great prize of the English throne.

From 1601-1603 James entered into a secret correspondence with Robert Cecil, Elizabeth's Secretary of State. Cecil's supporters controlled the army and James correctly supposed Cecil (who became James's chief minister in 1603) could secure his succession. There was no serious alternative candidate. In March 1603, three days after Elizabeth's death, a messenger from England brought the news to Holyrood: James VI of Scotland had become James I of England. As the delighted king prepared to journey south, he assured his Scots subjects, 'I shall visit you every three years or oftener as I shall have occasion.' He was to reign both kingdoms until his death in 1625 but his visit to Scotland in 1617 was the only one he made. The richer, more prestigious English court claimed all his attention and it is generally accepted that the development of Scottish culture was disastrously affected by the sudden and complete removal of royal patronage to London.

NOTE: STEWART or STUART?

I have chosen the convention of retaining the original Scots spelling of STEWART throughout this *Brief History*.

STEWART indicates descent from Walter, 3rd High Steward of Scotland, the husband of Robert I's daughter, Marjorie. Their son, Robert II (1316-1390) was the grandfather of James I (1394-1437).

STUART is very much a post-1603 development possibly for the benefit of the English and especially the French whose language has no 'w'.

Regal Union, 1603-1707

Quae Deus Convinxit Nemo Separet – What God has joined let no man separate.

Motto inscribed by James VI on the post-1603 crown piece

What were the implications for the people of Scotland of James's succession to the English throne? A common monarch would seem to promise the end of centuries of bloody conflict between England and Scotland, for kings declare war and how can a monarch declare war against himself? There never was another Anglo-Scottish battle after 1603. The main occasions when Scots and English soldiers opposed each other – Worcester (1651), Sherrifmuir (1715), Prestonpans (1745), Falkirk and Culloden (1746) – belonged technically to civil wars, not engagements between sovereign nations. War was, in fact, replaced by an increasing traffic of people and ideas between the two countries. Many Scots were inevitably drawn to London in James's wake. There they were exposed to English ways, speech and ideas. There were also advantages to be gained by Scotland from England's wide trading experience. However, the new situation wasn't without disadvantage for the Scots. England's superior wealth and size remained to threaten Scotland's cherished independence which had been achieved by years of bloody conflict. James himself was keen to make the Regal Union more complete and instructed commissioners to look into the possibility of a more extensive Union. Subsequent negotiations came to nothing because the English refused to grant Scots merchants full trading rights in England.

However, some positive steps were taken. The old laws which classified English and Scots as enemy aliens in each other's countries were replaced by the confirmation of rights of citizenship in England and Scotland for Scots and English born after the Regal Union. The earliest Union flag was created and a joint Anglo-Scottish body was instituted to bring law and order to the Borders, now called 'the Middle Shires'. James used the royal prerogative to create a new royal title which gives a good indication of his own aspirations. He chose to be referred to as 'the most high and mighty Prince, James by the Grace of God, King of Great Britain, France and Ireland'. He did not neglect to clarify his attitude towards the Highland culture of the country he effectively left behind in 1603.

> Forsamekle as, the Kingis Majestie haveing a speciall care and regaird that the trew religioun be advanceit and establisheit in all the pairtis of this kingdome, and that all his Majesties subjectis, especiallie the youth, be exercised and trayned up in civilitie, godlines, knawledge and learning, that the vulgar Inglishe toung be universallie plantit, and the Irish language, whilk is one of the cheif and principall causes of the continewance of barbaritie and incivilitie amongis the inhabitantis of the Isles and Heylandis, may be abolisheit and removit.

James VI & I, 1616

The neglect of Scotland continued with James's son Charles who, having left Scotland aged three, knew little about his northern kingdom. He had even stronger views than his father on the Divine Right of Kings which combined with his ignorance of the widespread strength of the Scottish Reformation to ignite the confrontations with the Parliaments of both countries and which led ultimately to his execution in 1648. He had initially provoked serious reaction in 1638 when his Scots subjects, infuriated by his arbitrary interference with their religion, formed a National Covenant to oppose the attempted religious innovations which he had sanctioned by Royal Prerogative. The Covenanters completed a successful military campaign against Charles, forcing him by 1640 to summon the English Parliament for the first time since 1629. He had been raising money since then by selling titles and using more forceful inducements. Now he needed more ready cash to carry on the fight in Scotland. Parliament relished this opportunity of imposing checks on monarchical power. Civil war between King and Parliament followed and both sides sought the help of the Scots who made, in 1643, an agreement with the English Parliament called the Solemn League and Covenant. In return for military assistance against Charles and his supporters, the English promised to protect Presbyterianism in Scotland and eventually to establish it in England. Scottish ranks excluded those who felt a strong allegiance to Charles as King of Scotland, among whom was Montrose, whom I had found so mysterious. He had been instrumental in establishing the Covenant but later became alienated from its extreme Presbyterian and anti-monarchical tendencies. He became Charles I's Commander in Scotland, winning many distinguished victories for the Royalist side. These were not enough to save Charles, however, and Montrose's defeat at Carbisdale in 1650 was probably inevitable after the King's execution.

By 1646, Charles's supporters had been overcome in Scotland and England but even the English revolutionaries proved that they were prepared to forget their promises to Scotland. Oliver Cromwell was now in control of the English Parliament. In 1647, a conservative element among the Covenanters tried to barter support for a beleaguered Charles in exchange for his establishment of Presbyterianism in both kingdoms. This outcome never materialised and Scottish forces were crushed by Cromwell's army at Preston in 1648. Many Scots, most notably Montrose, were genuinely shocked by Charles's execution in 1649 and made ready to fight for his son provided he accepted the Covenant. Cromwell inflicted decisive defeats on the Scottish army at Dunbar in 1650 and

Worcester in 1651. Scotland had no choice but to accept the English Lord Protector. Cromwell, now in control of England and Scotland, imposed a full Parliamentary Union between the two countries. Cromwell's parliamentary arrangements were never intended to provide much more than a rubber stamp for his military dictatorship. However, he introduced the pairing of the shires, Ross and Cromarty, Perth and Kinross which still survives. The Kirk went unmolested by Cromwell but mere toleration did not suit the Presbyterian majority. Most fiercely resented was the heavy taxation required to sustain the massive military presence in Scotland of the Lord Protector's forces which were centred on five large forts at Leith, Ayr, Perth, Inverlochy and Inverness.

When Cromwell died and his son, Richard, bowed out of politics, the Scots welcomed Charles II. They were ready after years of political and religious turmoil to accept him even as an absentee monarch. The Scottish Parliament met in 1661 and officially rescinded all legislation made since 1633. So Episcopacy was restored and both the Covenanting and Parliamentary Unions were forgotten. However, there were disappointing elements for Scots in the new arrangements. English legislation still excluded them from a share in England's burgeoning overseas trade. Despite Scottish resentment, the English were only to make significant trading concessions as part of a Union deal in which they gained complete strategic control of their northern neighbour and that was not to come for another fifty years.

Charles II was chiefly motivated in his restoration of Episcopacy by a desire for tolerance rather than any hostility towards Presbyterianism. Inevitably, the Presbyterian extremists, the Cameronians, who wanted nothing less than the total re-establishment of Presbyterianism, came into conflict with Charles's policy. However, militarily they were impotent against superior government forces. (The Cameronians became the

Reformed Presbyterians in 1743 and in 1876 most of them united with the Free Church of Scotland.)

1688 saw the re-establishment in Scotland of Presbyterianism (with provision for some toleration) by William III who had been brought from Holland to rule England and Scotland with his wife, James II's daughter, Mary, after the Glorious Revolution of the same year. James II, Charles II's brother, had been welcomed as King after Charles's death despite his Roman Catholicism. However, his religious tactlessness alienated many Scots when he asked the London Parliament to grant toleration to Roman Catholics. The security of the Protestant faith was of prime consideration for both Scottish and English Parliaments. James's ineptitude in this context and the birth of his son in 1688 made his replacement inevitable.

So William was welcomed as the saviour of Protestant England and Scotland. The only serious support for James II was in the Highlands where John Graham of Claverhouse, Viscount Dundee, received James's commission to raise the clans on his behalf. At the head of three thousand Highlanders he defeated government forces under General Mackay at the Battle of Killiecrankie in 1689, but Bonnie Dundee was killed in the battle and the rebellion failed. A symbol of William's triumph and his determination to keep the rebellious north in order was the erection of Fort William which the government built at Inverlochy in 1690.

William's reign defined the unmistakably inferior role of Scotland within the Regal Union. Two incidents occurring at different sides of the globe illustrated this vividly. The first and most notorious was closely linked to Fort William. In an attempt to subdue completely the restless Highlanders, efforts were made by the government to induce the Jacobite chiefs to declare their support for William and Mary. A Royal Pardon for former disloyalty to the throne was offered in 1691 as the reward for such public avowal of support but any failure to make such an avowal was to be severely punished. Alexander MacDonald of Glencoe was chief of a clan already singled out for harsh punishment by one of the King's Scots advisers in London, Sir John Dalyrimple, Master of Stair. He felt the troublesome Highlanders should be taught a terrible lesson for their disloyalty in 1689. He described the Glencoe MacDonalds as 'a damnable sect, the worst in the Highlands' and had 'determined to take a severe course with them'. The Highlanders, despite Cromwell's military penetration of their territory and William's defeat of James II's supporters, still lived very much as they had been doing for centuries, organised in clans which felt far more active loyalty to their chief than to any London monarch. Even the Lowlands of Scotland were remote and essentially foreign to them. *A Description of the Western Isles of Scotland* by Martin Martin (1693) includes this first-hand account of Raasay. Dr Samuel Johnson had been given this book by his father as a child. It had inspired his journey to the Highlands and Islands in 1773.

> The proprietor of the isle is Mr MacLeod, a cadet of the family of that name; his seat is in the village Clachan. The inhabitants have as great veneration for him as any subjects can have for their king.

Alexander MacDonald of Glencoe tried to take the oath of loyalty demanded by the Crown but bureaucratic delay, intentional or otherwise, delayed his submission until January 1692, after the government deadline. The King, whose precise knowledge of the local situation and, therefore, whose ultimate responsibility for what happened is not clear, then issued instructions to 'extirpate that sect of thieves'.

The planned massacre was carried out on 6 February by enemies of the MacDonalds, the Campbells of Glen Lyon. Colonel Hill, the garrison commander at Inverlochy had especially chosen them for the job and ordered that they should be billeted on the MacDonalds. The massacre, therefore, contravened the revered code of Highland hospitality and revolt at the slaughter (thirty-eight MacDonalds, including women and children, were killed by the Campbells) spread throughout Scotland and England. News of the event was seized upon by opponents of William and his government who denounced the slaughter on moral as well as political grounds. Yet no action was taken by the government to gain redress for the atrocity until 1695 when the only significant result of an enquiry was the removal of the Master of Stair from his government position. A century before, the death of less than forty obscure Highlanders in the never-ending tally of inter-clan strife would have been unremarkable but public opinion was more sensitive now. The belief that the government had instigated the plan was a clear indication that Highlanders were not seen by Westminster to deserve better treatment than the savages the British Navy was now discovering on distant shores.

The second incident so indicative of Scotland's disadvantaged position in the Regal Union happened in 1695 and belonged not to the ancient world of clan warfare but to the utterly modern one of expanding global trade. Scottish business interests, hoping to emulate the remarkable successes of the English East India Company (founded in 1600) in its trading with the newly-discovered colonies, inspired the Scottish Parliament in 1695 to pass an Act creating a Scottish company to trade with Africa and the Indies. Initially the project was to obtain half its capital from London and London financiers, eager for a share in the projected profits, were to make up half the Board of Directors. However, the English Parliament forbade any English involvement in the scheme under pressure from the English East India Company which wanted to keep its monopoly on eastern trade. The Scots decided on Darien in Panama as the site for their enterprise. This was part of a territory claimed by Spain, and William III was anxious to avoid Spain's enmity because of the claims of England's arch-rival, France, to the Spanish succession. The English Navy, therefore, was instructed to withhold any assistance from the colonists. The Scots refused to be discouraged and the project attracted widespread popular support.

In retrospect, one feels a dreadful sense of doom hanging over the whole endeavour. The first expedition arrived in Darien in 1698 (with insufficient provisions) and discovered the deadly nature of the local climate. The news of attacks by the Spanish and the high toll of illness did not reach Scotland in time to prevent the second and third expeditions embarking. The colonists were able to repulse Spanish aggression at first but by 1700 they were finally forced to evacuate their settlement. Many of the colonists died on their way home and the Scottish economy was seriously weakened by the loss of the capital which had been invested in the company.

Parliamentary Union, 1707 – ?

Fareweel to a' our Scottish fame,
Fareweel our ancient glory;
Fareweel even to the Scottish name,
Sae famed in martial story!

From A *Parcel of Rogues*, contemporary Scottish song, later made famous by Robert Burns

Many Scots blamed English policies for the failure of the Darien scheme. More importantly, the contradictions of a Regal Union were highlighted by this episode in which Scots and English interests clashed so markedly. The situation seemed to suggest to pragmatists on both sides of the Border that a more practical and effective arrangement than Regal Union must be sought. But why should the English feel obliged to enter into constructive arrangements with the northern neighbours that they were still intent on subjugating even if in a different, 18th century context? The answer of course is based on English self-interest, albeit a more sophisticated sort of self-interest than the brutal power-politics of Edward I. It is, therefore, worth identifying precisely English motives in the years leading up to Parliamentary Union in 1707. They explain much about the actual experience of the Union since it began and, therefore, much of the basis for the modern relationship between the English and the Scots.

The politicians who carried England into the Act of Union were influenced by one set of considerations which had been in operation since the mid-16th century and another set which were to dominate English, and then British history until after the Second World War and are not altogether defunct today. The first set, based on the importance of securing the Protestant religion, had originated with Henry VIII's adoption of Protestantism in 1529. This had grown into a determination to protect England and its Reformation against the vividly-perceived threat of Catholic attack (notably from France and Spain) on England, its religion and its crown. It was this fear which had led Elizabeth to order her cousin Mary's execution and had inspired the perpetrators of the Glorious Revolution in 1689 to give the Catholic James II's throne to his Protestant son-in-law and daughter. James II and VII was the last Stewart King and the last Catholic King of England. His name (or the Latin version of it) was given to the two last attempts to replace the ruling monarch: the Jacobite Rebellions of 1715 and 1745.

The Act of Settlement in 1701 was a striking example of the English establishment's total determination to exclude Catholics from the English and Scottish thrones. The Act laid down a law which still stands, though reported to be under review by the government at the time of writing. It makes Catholics 'forever incapable to inherit, possess or enjoy the Crown of or government of this realm.' It is a measure of the extreme strength of the ruling élite's anti-Catholic purpose that the Hanoverian Succession, which was enabled by the Act, passed the throne to a physically unattractive German man who spoke little English, over the heads of at least fifty individuals who were dynastically closer to Queen Anne but who were disqualified from consideration by their Catholicism. Bishop Richard Willis wrote in 1715, 'A Protestant country can never have stable times under a Popish Prince any more than a flock of sheep can have quiet when a wolf is their shepherd.'

Protestantism had developed a particularly crucial importance in England by this time. Major developments of the 17th century, such as the growing power of Parliament, the final rejection of the Stewarts and the impressive start of a colonial empire, all seemed to imply that Protestant England had been especially chosen by God as a sort of modern-day Israel. Although church attendance remained moderate, most literate households had a copy of *Foxe's Book of Martyrs* (which had been continuously in print since 1563) as well as *Pilgrim's Progress*, an allegorical attack on the anti-Christ of the Roman Church.

One important result of this burgeoning sense of Protestant identity was that it made Union with Scotland eminently imaginable. The Scottish Reformation of 1560 had involved the majority of the population, the main Catholic remnant being some of the Highland clans. However, the politics of militant Protestantism had another more important effect on England's relationship with Scotland. Just twenty-two miles from England's south coast lay that aspect of the anti-Christ represented by Catholic France. There were always going to be the strong geopolitical reasons of size and proximity to fear France. The Counter-Reformation had merely given an extra intensity to the long-established territorial rivalry between England and France.

The frequent, severe famines experienced in France in the second half of the 17th century seemed to confirm the idea of England having some sort of divine advantage as did the absolutist inefficiency of the Bourbon monarchy. The Auld Alliance with France had been Scotland's traditional response to the constant threat of its overbearing neighbour, although it is important to remember it was only an intermittent alliance. Nevertheless, the threat of French invasion through the back door of Scotland's extensive coastline was a powerful motive for England to proceed with an incorporating Union.

There was another reason to worry about the French. A second set of English considerations which favoured a closer link with Scotland were part of the wholly modern concern for the security of the growing English colonial Empire. By 1700, England had valuable territories in America and India and the main threat to their security came from French territorial ambitions in those regions. The potential rewards of the nascent Empire were now simply too high to allow Scotland's Auld Alliance to jeopardise them. Scotland must be made safe and there was no overwhelming cultural obstacle to prevent a Union between the two countries.

By 1705, the contradictions of the Regal Union were impossible to ignore. The English Parliament, for all the reasons just outlined, was determined to secure the Hanoverian succession. The Scottish Parliament tried to bargain with its English counterpart, making its acceptance of the Hanoverian succession conditional on guarantees of security for the Scottish crown and for freedom of Scottish religion and trade. The English Parliament, unable to tolerate any uncertainty over their plans for the succession, passed the Alien Act in 1705. This decreed that unless Scots accepted the succession to both thrones of George Lewis of Hanover (great-grandson of James VI and I) they would be treated by England as foreigners. This would mean that Scottish cattle, coal and linen could no longer be

exported to the all-important English market. The English
Parliament simultaneously proposed the setting up of a closer Union
between the two countries. Scotland was therefore given little
option to refuse yet another English rough wooing. In any event, the
disastrous financial effects of the Darien scheme meant that the
Scots had to take every step possible to improve their economic
prospects. Unrestricted trade with England and her growing
colonies was simply too good an opportunity to miss.
Commissioners from both countries proceeded to draft a Treaty of
Union which attempted to weld the antagonisms and requirements
of both countries into a workable arrangement. The Scottish
Parliament spent the winter of 1706-1707 in extensive discussions
and the Treaty was signed in May 1707.

How much of what each side wanted did it get? English
dynastic and security concerns were satisfied by the dissolution of
the Scottish Parliament. Scotland was granted Free Trade with
England and her colonies and obtained a significant transfer of
money to compensate Scotland for sharing the burden of the
English National Debt. Scots law and the Kirk were guaranteed
survival but the new arrangements for Scottish representation at
Westminster were less than satisfactory. The English commission
had linked representation with taxation and so Scotland's smaller
revenues meant fewer MPs and Peers. It was not until 1832 that
this discrepancy was addressed.

Given the oligarchic nature of 18th century government it is
unhistorical to wonder how a deal which was unpopular in
England and deeply resented by a majority of Scots (news of the
signing of the Union was greeted by hostile rioting all over
Scotland) could have been accomplished. The account of events
given in the contemporary song, *Such a Parcel of Rogues in a
Nation*, provides an accurate enough analysis of the pragmatic
workings of 18th century power-politics:

What force or guile could not subdue
Thro' many warlike ages,
Is wrought now by a coward few
For hireling traitors' wages.

England and Scotland may have had centuries of bitter conflict behind them but at the dawn of the 18th century, that gateway to the modern era of western democracy and global economics, they shared one very important characteristic: they were both ruled by aristocratic oligarchies. The governors of both countries had far more in common with each other than with the lower orders within their own country's boundaries. The Act of Union was a back-room deal done between these two ruling élites. The English rulers were concerned with achieving security and prosperity for their own country thereby strengthening their own position significantly. The Scottish Parliament took a whole winter of debate to agree to its own abolition but in the end the personal advantages of money and position in the new Great Britain was simply too persuasive for the majority of the Scottish ruling élite, the *'Parcel of Rogues'*, to resist.

The part played by the Duke of Hamilton in the debates leading directly to the passing of the Act of Union and the Scottish Parliament's self-abolition is a good example of the way Scots anti-Union sentiment, despite widespread popular (often violent) support, was compromised by the personal considerations of key Scottish individuals. Having been the darling of the anti-Unionist Edinburgh mob at the start of the six months of debate and negotiations preceding the Union, the Duke, like many other Scots magnates, was eventually convinced of the economic benefits the Union would bring Scotland and, in particular, its ruling class. He therefore discouraged the strangely-allied Jacobite and Cameronian rebellion against the Union. He had originally supported a popular deputation demanding that a new Scottish Parliament might be given the chance to express widespread Scottish misgivings about the Union. He had also backed the plans of anti-Union members of the Scottish Parliament to withdraw their support for the Union unless Scottish representation in the incorporated parliament was increased. The plan had widespread popular support. However, at the last minute, pretending to be seized by the toothache, Hamilton suddenly decided to withhold his support. Like many Scots magnates, he was motivated by that self-interest which had always played a major role in the history of the Scottish nobility. This group was very often more concerned with its own ends than any idea of national advantage. These inevitable aspirations within Scotland's ruling class combined with her poverty to minimise the chances of her resisting English plans for Union.

So, the Union stands at a notional mid-point between the days when Edward I used England's superior military strength to bully Scotland into submitting to his plans of feudal conquest and the present when the Union has come to be seen more and more as an arbitrary political anachronism.

Still we can't, having gone into this much detail, jump from 1707 to 1997 although it is probably safe to say that events of this final period are more familiar to most of us than the violent complications of early Scottish history. However, it's perhaps worth an attempt to forestall any criticism of my analysis of the making of the Union as too sketchy and too inclined to substitute the words of an old ballad for detailed historical and critical analysis. Well, in as much as we are examining the history of Anglo-Scots relationship to throw light on its present state, the survival of that song and its inclusion by Burns in his first *Kilmarnock Edition* gives its analysis of the Union at least the status of generally agreed contemporary opinion, if not exact historical truth. The 18th century English manipulated the Scots with money and promises of position just as Edward I had done with his armies in the 13th century. Both types of domination were dependent on England's superior material position over Scotland which meant England could always be the big brother that Scotland never managed to equal for long enough to significantly change the score. Now we must look to see what followed the legalisation of England's *de facto* dominion.

Scottish popular dissatisfaction showed itself regularly in the decades following the Union: rioting against Westminster's increases of tax on beer and spirits were frequent occurrences and protests against the new taxes were often joined with chants of 'No Union, No Union'.

The Jacobite Rebellion and its Consequences

What a spectacle of horror! The same Highlanders who had advanced to the charge like lions, with bold and determined countenance, were in an instant seen flying like trembling cowards in the greatest disorder

Memoir of the Forty-five, Chevalier de Johnstone

Inevitably, the Jacobites were opposed to the Union which was, remember, in part a measure to safeguard the Hanoverian Succession. The power of Jacobite protest after the Union was seriously weakened by the failure of their Catholic allies' continental armies to deliver military help to the Jacobites as well as by consistently poor leadership among the Jacobites themselves. 1708 and 1719 saw two ineffectual Jacobite risings. The '15 and the '45 were of a more serious nature.

The '15 was as much to do with the thwarted political ambitions of its formerly pro-Union leader, the Earl of Mar, as with Jacobite fervour. His faulty leadership and the woeful timing of

James II's son, the Old Pretender, meant that English troops had little trouble suppressing the rising. The next serious rising, the '45, lasted nine months and at one stage came sufficiently far south to throw the English capital into a panic. The '45 did, however, have a serious historical legacy despite its inevitable failure. To understand this legacy we must remember that the Union's main purpose had been to achieve dynastic and territorial security for England. The Jacobite rebellion of 1745 seemed to justify all the fears that had motivated the Union. Though ultimately ineffectual, the promise of French help had inspired this rebellion and much of London's fears. Charles Edward Stewart, the Young Pretender, had, from the outset, been determined to seize the thrones of Scotland and England for the Stewart dynasty.

The clan was not just the tribe but the children of the chief. Charles Edward Stewart was the supreme receptacle for the clansmen's loyalty, trust and devotion. The bards were busy in 1745 and 1746, as was the custom, inciting the clan to war and then expressing the bitter, defeated defiance which was felt by them after Culloden. The following is an extract from the *Song of the Highland Clans*, 1745.

> Many will the spoilers be
> Of corpses on the field,
> Ravens will be cawing there,
> Fluttering, and sauntering,
> Kites a-feeding rav'nously
> To eat and drink their fill;
> O, sad and faint at morn will rise
> The cries of those who fell.
>
> Blood and gore will mingled be
> By your dext'rous hands,
> Heads and fists will be lopped off,
> Bones broken, and joints hacked apart,

Your foemen will be overwhelmed,
Fire-blackened, and consumed;
Charles Stewart with glory will be crowned,
Prince Frederick trampled down.

Alexander MacDonald, translated from the Gaelic by John Lorne Campbell

Had Charles been content to do so, he might have been able to secure Scotland alone against English recapture, thereby creating a highly insecure northern frontier for England as she attempted to consolidate her colonial position. I emphasise these aspects of the '45 to account for the brutal nature of the revenge that the Duke of Cumberland inflicted on the Highlands after the '45 was crushed at the Battle of Culloden in the spring of 1746. This is an extract from *A Song to the Britches*:

And now 'tis we who surely know
The mercy that Duke William's shown,
Since he's left us like prisoners
Without our dirks, without our guns,
Without our belts, without our swords,
We may not even pistols have,
For England has command of us
Since she did wholly conquer us;
There's anger too and misery
In many a man now at this time,
Who was in William's camp before
Who's now no better that he's won;
And if Prince Charles to us returned
We would rise and follow him,
The scarlet plaids once more be worn
And all the guns be out again.

Duncan Ban MacIntyre, translated from the Gaelic by John Lorne Campbell

The aftermath of Culloden is frequently condensed and sanitised by emphasising the adventures of Charles Edward Stewart as he tried to evade the English army in order to escape to France. In this version, as a sort of moral consolation prize to the Highland population, much is made of the fact that, despite the huge price promised for his capture by the Government, Charles was not betrayed by any of the Highlanders who sheltered him (at great risk to themselves) before his escape. Conversely and more deplorably, what is often left out of the accounts of Culloden's aftermath is the genocidal campaign of vengeful attrition which Cumberland initiated. In August 1747, Cumberland left for England but the naval frigate, HMS Furnace, executed his punitive policy with devastating ferocity along the western seaboard. His victory at Culloden had exposed the Highlands and Islands to the full military force of a Westminster government for the first time. Like those it purported to represent, the Government hated and feared a culture which seemed alien and savage and had proved capable of giving it a good fright. No opportunity to exact revenge on the Highlands was, therefore, neglected.

Now this long journey through the history of the relationship between Scotland and England has reached a point where specific events are still alive in the memory of Highlanders. Raasay is a compelling example of what happened to the Gaels after Culloden and how it has lived on in the Highland memory. The Stewart Prince stayed on Raasay during his flight from the English army. This meant the island was to receive special attention from the English military. Every house was destroyed by fire as were all the boats. Opposite Raasay on the mainland of Wester Ross at the beginning of the 1990s, John Macleod, author of *No Great Mischief if You Fall*, a moving account of some of the history of the Gaels, met someone whose family's memories included the sight of Raasay burning after the visit from HMS Furnace.

This military offensive against the Gaidhealtachd was followed by a legislative dismantling of the clan structure. All Highland clans were affected even though many, including the Campbells, Munros and some of the MacLeods, had not come out for the Jacobite cause. The Disarming Act and Heritable Jurisdiction Act (1747) were radically responsible for undermining the clan system and the whole socio-political landscape of the Highlands. Up to the time of Culloden, a chief's land did not provide him with a cash income from rents but with a tally of fighting men, officered by tacksmen. These tacksmen leased their land to sub-tenants whose rent was paid in kind and who would follow tacksmen and chief into battle on the latter's command. The lowest position in the clan hierarchy belonged to the landless cottar who paid for his stone hut and patch of ground by working as servant to the tacksman. All these clansmen regarded themselves as the children of their chief to whom their loyalty was complete. Culloden marked the beginning of the end of this patriarchal clan system. The Heritable Jurisdiction Act destroyed the power of the chiefs to administer justice within the clan and the Disarming Act criminalised the Highlanders' traditional identity with the carrying of weapons being made illegal as well as the wearing of the kilt. The bagpipes, those 'engines of war' as they were loathingly described by the English, were also banned.

The Clearances

They want fine fields and fine forests; what care they for men?

Thomas MacLauchlan, Presbyterian Divine and Gaelic scholar

Charles Edward died, aged 68, in France, but his metamorphosis from dashing young leader of the '45 to disillusioned drunk is merely one man's pathetic, disappointed decline. The effect of the doomed rebellion on the whole Highland population was to end their way of life forever by destroying the social system on which it was based. The importance of Culloden and its aftermath, including the abandonment by the clan chiefs of their patriarchal responsibilities, is minimised by some historians with the assertion that the development of the cash economy and subsequent Agricultural and Industrial Revolutions would in any case have doomed the clans' traditional way of life. While acknowledging this, it is important to emphasise the precise legacy of the events connected with and proceeding from Culloden. Cumberland's brutality at and after Culloden was systematic and appalling. The clan chiefs, both loyal and Jacobite, in subsequent decades behaved with a more subtle, though equally destructive, cruelty towards their clansmen. Shorn of their traditional powers and responsibilities, they transformed themselves into aristocrats on a contemporary European model. So, while the end of the old ways was inevitable, the extreme harshness of the Highlanders' eventual fate constituted a cultural genocide and made the modern-day Highlands an empty memorial to this betrayal.

As the generation of those chieftains who had fought (or not) at Culloden died out, their successors, deprived of their politico-legal function by the Heritable Jurisdictions Act, turned south for an alternative role model. They discovered that to emulate the English land-owning aristocracy they required quantities of ready cash for luxurious clothes, town houses in Edinburgh and London, foreign travel, educations for their sons and significant dowries for their daughters. A tally of fighting men was worthless in this context: the chiefs' lands must be made to yield cash. The trend towards agricultural improvement was already established in England and its methods provided the cash-hungry chiefs with a simple answer to their problems: all they had to do was change their land use fundamentally. This was most profitably done by replacing their tenants with sheep which were brought to the Highlands in their hundreds of thousands accompanied by shepherds from northern England and the Scottish Lowlands with names like Hunter, Armstrong and Elliot.

As the century progressed, this tide of economic change swept away the social cohesion over which the chieftains had presided. Some of those evicted to make way for cattle pastures and then sheep walks were settled on the coast: an alien environment where the lessons of making a living from the sea had to be learnt from scratch at the cost of very survival. Many more of those turned off the land emigrated to Canada, America and Australia. At the end of the 18th century some of the better-off tacksmen could afford to organise their Atlantic crossing in relative comfort and safety and were able to arrive well-equipped to make the most of the opportunities provided by their new home. But there were many among the evicted tenantry who did not enjoy such advantages.

Archibald Geikie, eminent geologist, visited Skye as a young student in the 1850s. He saw some evicted tenants leaving their homes for the last time and included the scene in his memoirs:

> When they set forth once more, a cry of grief went up to heaven, the long plaintive wail, like a funeral coronach, was resumed, and after the last of the emigrants had disappeared behind the hill, the sound seemed to re-echo through the whole wide valley... in one prolonged note of desolation.

The voyages could be expensive, dangerous and exhausting and many of the poorer tenants who were fortunate enough to survive them, and many weren't, arrived at their distant destination sickly and destitute. This is certainly a well-known if shameful episode in the history of the Highlands. The unthinking obedience of the clansmen to their chief exposed some to the brutality of Hanoverian revenge and then the majority to inhuman betrayal by the men they loved and respected as fathers. The displaced tenantry could only acquiesce in their chiefs' designs: their inherited world-view left them no choice but to do so. I include two contemporary comments here, one from a Gael, John MacCodrum, and one from an Englishman, Dr Samuel Johnson.

MacCodrum was bard to Sir Alexander MacDonald of Uist. John Prebble in his 1963 classic, *The Highland Clearances*, includes this translation of MacCodrum's bitter protest against the actions of his particular landlord:

> Look around you and see the nobility without pity for poor folk, without kindness to friends; they are of the opinion that you do not belong to the soil, and though they have left you destitute they cannot see it as a loss; they have lost sight of every law and promise that was observed by the men who took this land from the foe: but let them tell me whether they will not lose their right to it, without means of saving it, when you go into exile.

Dr Johnson stopped on Raasay during his Highland tour of 1773. Here he summed up his observations of the Highland chieftains as follows:

> They gradually degenerate from patriarchal rulers to rapacious landlords; [and] divest themselves of what little [dignity] remains... Where there was formerly an insurrection there is now a wilderness.

The growing power of the British state with its ambition for global territorial acquisitions and its expanding industrial economy was responsible for two key aspects of the way the Highlands' economic development proceeded in the second half of the 18th century. The first of these major developments reversed the post-Culloden suppression of the military prowess and energies of the Highland clans. Sir Robert Walpole, in 1725, had approved the enrolment of loyal clansmen to patrol the Highlands. They dressed in tartan of sombre colours and so became known as The Black Watch, a name they kept when they were formed into a regiment in 1739. After the '45, London's furious hatred of the Highlanders meant the thousands of fighting men left redundant by the post-Culloden pacification were simply not considered for British military service. This policy came to an end in the Seven Years War against France (1756-1763) when William Pitt, the Elder, sanctioned the levying of Highland Regiments which were to perform such notable services in the establishment and defence of the British Empire and beyond to the World Wars of the next century.

> I am for having always in our army as many Scottish soldiers as possible, not that I think them more brave than those of any other country we can recruit from, but because they are generally more hardy and less mutinous: and of all Scottish soldiers I would choose to have and keep in our army as many Highlanders as possible.

> Secretary of War, Lord Barrington speaking to Parliament, 1751

By the last quarter of the 18th century, Scottish society was finally reaping the benefits of the Union. England had needed the Union to remove the threat of a treacherous Scotland at her back as she pursued her Imperial ambitions. By 1780, despite the disastrous loss of the American colonies, English power was securely established against the French threat in Canada and India and the Scots, including the Highland Regiments, had made an important contribution to this Imperial effort.

> At a battle in defence of Quebec in 1760, General James Murray commanded a mixed force of English regiments and Highlanders. It appears that at the outset, he ordered the pipers not to play, but later, when the Highlanders were being beaten back one of their officers went so far as to protest that the General had been wrong and that even yet the pipers might be of use. Sure enough, the pipers being ordered to play a favourite

cruinneachadh, the Highlanders, who were broken, returned and formed with great alacrity.

J Ramsay, 1784, quoted in *The Highland Bagpipe and its Music*, Roderick D Cannon

The resulting agglomeration of territory, the British Empire, though its capital was in London, was never referred to as the English Empire. England had forced Scotland to abandon any independent powers which might jeopardise this vast territorial project. In return, Scots were allowed to join in and benefit from the Imperial enterprise which they did often with great distinction as soldiers, sailors, diplomats, administrators, explorers and traders. The Highlanders, in particular, were taken from their own defeated world and employed in the up-to-date fighting machine which was to become the British Imperial army of the 19th century. Yet this development made little direct contribution to modernising the Highlands or raising living standards there.

The Sporting Estates

The English sportsmen would be shooting in our corn. The women who would be quietly herding would have to fly home for fear of bullets.

(Evidence given by Skye crofter to the Napier Commission)

Another major trend radically to affect the Highlands developed in the following century and proceeded directly from the spectacular economic progress experienced by the south of Scotland and England in a century of massive industrial activity. The sporting estate is a living link in the historical chain of the Anglo-Scots power relationship which started with Edward 1's aggression and progressed *via* the Union and Culloden to the anglicisation of the Highland chiefs and the subsequent Clearances. For many Highlanders that chain of events meant eventual dispossession and exile to either industrial Scotland or the distant colonies. The rise and contemporary survival of the sporting estate stands as perhaps the ultimate monument to the extreme distortions these political changes had on land values, use and distribution in the Highlands.

Early Scottish monarchs had pursued game in their Royal Hunting Forests but by the 18th century there were only half a dozen or so of these areas left in the Highlands. Immense changes were to occur in Highland land use over the next one hundred and fifty years as landed estates, run by their owners for the chief purpose of providing hunting opportunities for the well-to-do, became all too common in Scotland as the following table shows:

Year	Acreage of Sporting Estates in Scotland
1900	2.5m
1906	3.5m
1957	2.8m

(Based on Andy Wightman's figures in *Who Owns Scotland* Canongate, 1996)

The very existence of these estates has come to represent the worst abuses of land ownership in Scotland itself which could be the reason that no figures are available for later than 1957. Some crucial factors led to this proliferation of the sporting estate. First, industrial and agricultural activity in England and the south of Scotland had widely damaged the rural environment there and so significantly reduced its sporting value. For example, new harvesting machinery left stubble fields close-cut thus reducing essential cover for wildfowl. Many wildlife habitats had also been seriously harmed by industrial pollution. This caused a distinct reduction in sporting opportunities in southern Scotland and England. The second important factor here is the decline in profitability of the sheep walks which had been established after the eviction of thousands of tenants throughout the Highlands in the century following Culloden. Land unsuited to such use had been intensively grazed for over a century which had led to a sharp decline in its fertility. In addition, by 1880, cheap lamb and mutton was arriving from Australia and New Zealand in new refrigerated ships. Those countries were also exporting wool to Britain. Highland landowners, therefore, had to find another source of income and the sale or rent of their lands to disgruntled English sportsmen provided the perfect solution for them. Queen Victoria established a Royal residence at Balmoral on Deeside which she had first visited in 1848. This move to the Highlands was copied extensively, though not always on quite such a lavish scale, by successful capitalists from all over Britain. Her husband, Prince Albert, though not a brilliant shot, was a very keen sportsman thus investing Highland sporting activity with a Royal glamour.

> ...a great herd [of deer were] running down a good way, when, most provokingly two men who were walking on the road – which they had no business to have done - suddenly came in sight and then the herd all ran back again, and the sport was spoiled.

> Queen Victoria's diary, describing Albert's attempts to shoot deer during a visit to Perthshire in 1844

So, much of the Highlands were turned into a sporting playground for the monied classes of England and the rest of Europe. Estates in the west of the Highlands were more usually managed for stalking deer and those in the east for shooting pheasant and grouse.

This chronology has been detailed enough to excuse the reader for forgetting its main purpose. But the sporting estate, standing as a direct result of the 18th century chief's transformation from patriarch to modern capitalist landowner also plays a crucial contemporary role in shaping the perceived identity of the English in the Highlands and this has happened in various ways.

Many of the sporting estates are owned by individuals or companies from outwith Scotland. The Scots who do own sporting estates tend to belong to the Anglo-Scots establishment. The close links of this Anglo-Scots property-owning network has been described by Andy Wightman in his admirable book, *Who Owns Scotland* (Canongate, 1996) as has its connections to the English ruling establishment *via* institutions such as international banking, the National Trust for Scotland and the extended British Royal Family. The complicated ties of property and kinship he documents in his very impressive analysis of current ownership patterns in Scotland have been evolving since at least 1707. Indeed links between Scots and English landowning classes go back a long way. The descendants of Malcolm Canmore invited English nobles to take over lands in Scotland and so to strengthen the monarchy with their feudal support. Marriage between the aristocracies on each side of the Border has been happening ever since with a definite increase after 1707. There are also quite a few sporting estate owners who come from outside the United Kingdom but the special place held by the English in Scotland's hall of landowning infamy is confirmed by one of Mr Wightman's invaluable tables. It is an analysis of the geographical origins of approximately four thousand members of the Scottish Landowners' Federation (based on their home address by country). England, which is treated as a region like the individual Scottish counties, actually comes fourth of thirty-eight areas of origin with one hundred and ninety-six members. Further down the list, with fourteen members, is the general category of members from outwith the British Isles.

So why is the ownership of sporting estates so important? Are these estates not simply a collection of quaint, irrelevant anachronisms? Rather, from the all-important perspective of rural development, the sporting estates represent a powerfully negative presence in contemporary Scotland. The vitality of the countryside is crucially important not just to those who live there but also to society as a whole. Sporting estates represent exactly the wrong sort of land use for constructive, sustainable and generally sensitive rural development. In relation to the acres they cover, these estates support very few workers who tend to be poorly paid or only seasonally employed. Most sporting estates do not make a profit and are in fact often run by their extremely wealthy owners at a loss for tax reasons: the only concrete advantage to be obtained from what must be the last word in late 20th century conspicuous consumption. Yet the consequences for rural development are dire. The demand for sporting estates means land prices are pushed way over their productive value which bars local individuals or communities from being able to afford constructive access to the land and its resources. It's as if the ostentatious whims of an essentially foreign (to the Highlands, if not to Scotland as a whole) élite are holding huge chunks of Scotland in suspended animation, governed by the rules and objectives of a neo-Victorian plutocracy.

> Sporting estates tend to be valued not on the land but on the price people are willing to pay to catch salmon or shoot stags on the sprawling properties.
>
> In 1990, these charges averaged £1300 per fish and £3000 per stag.
>
> *Herald*, 25 February 1997

By definition, these estates require the most rigid nature conservation and, therefore, they are most likely to oppose sustainable, people-centred rural development. Anyone with an all-round concern for the Highlands will tell you about the immense damage done to the natural environment by the huge deer population. Moreover, the contemporary importance of the sporting estates goes far beyond these questions of local land use. The Highlands have a symbolic importance for the rest of Scotland dating at least from the significant Lowland support the Skye crofters attracted in their battle for land rights in the 1880s. Many Scots have family roots in the Highlands and most are aware of the unique environmental status of the area. It must, therefore, for most Scots, be galling in the extreme to see so much of this special place locked up in foreign control beyond the financial reach of local individuals or communities or indeed almost anybody but the non-indigenous super-rich.

A frequent defence of the sporting estates is that the land they occupy is too poor to be used for anything else. This argument is contradicted by the experience of similar areas in Europe which have been managed more constructively and with much more concern for local communities. Denmark is a good example here. Its rural uplands feature plenty of well thought-out sustainable projects, like community forestry, which provide jobs and housing. As a result they do not experience the rural depopulation endemic in many Highland areas.

Of course, the very existence of the sporting estates as well as their ownership by outsiders and non-UK citizens reflects a specific government policy on land ownership. This policy is certainly, in its attitude to foreign ownership and its apparent lack of positive interest in land-based rural development, very different from that of many other European countries. As Andy Wightman wryly points out, UK Overseas Development Aid would not be granted to a rural area bound by such anachronistic and inegalitarian land regulations. The state of political affairs which permits the existence of the sporting estates would surely never be tolerated by an independent Scottish Parliament. Although there is still a century or so of this chronology to run increasingly what history remains is characterised by demands for greater control by Scotland of her own destiny. The thuggery and compulsion of the preceding attempts to hold Scotland in the *de facto* submission of its more powerful southern neighbour is replaced by a more subtle political process of procrastination and evasion. Violence and coercion declines but there remains a guiding determination to maintain the *status quo* that is the Union.

The depression in sheep farming intensified the inevitable conflict between the crofters and the management of sporting estates. These two land uses were indeed mutually antagonistic. We return to Raasay for an illustration. Here rabbits, the bane of any farmer's life, were actually protected for sport by Herbert Wood, the landowner whose family owned and controlled Raasay from 1876 to 1912. He came to the Highlands from Suffolk having originally made his fortune as an industrial magnate in the Staffordshire potteries. The land which previous owners had cleared for sheep he gave over to deer, pheasants and the dreaded rabbits. Wood stopped rabbit trappers from coming to Raasay to carry out their regular culls. The sole purpose of his innovations was to enhance the sporting opportunities of the estate. No prizes for guessing whose sport! The crofters were forbidden to protect their land in any way which harmed the rabbits or other game which belonged to the laird. We get a detailed impression of the sort of problems this caused in practice from evidence given by crofters to the Napier Commission:

> I was three years that I could not put a seed into the ground with the deer

> They [the deer] are so vicious – more so than deer I see anywhere else – that they twist themselves between the wires to get at the corn.

> We are so much pressed by tacksmen on both sides and behind by sportsmen and their keepers that we are not allowed to walk without the fear of being taken up as trespassers.

Some of us walking up our own pasture have been threatened that if we did they would put lead in our bodies.

The resentment of the Highland tenantry finally exploded in 1882 when the Crofters' War broke out on Skye, then spread to the Outer Isles and the western seaboard. Landlords attempted to arrest and even evict the protesting crofters and were supported by the police and occasionally by gunboats and Marines. But from Martinmas 1883, a crofters' rent strike went ahead. Meanwhile, the Napier Commission was appointed by the Liberal Government to examine the crofters' case and in 1886, following the Commission's not unsympathetic report, Parliament passed the Crofters' Holdings Act. This established fair rents, security of tenure and guaranteed compensation for any improvements made by crofters to their croft. Thus the crofters' main grievances were satisfied and the rent arrears which had accumulated during the strike were cancelled.

The Crofters' War showed to the whole of Scotland the scope of improvements which could be implemented by a legislature made up of Scots and based in Scotland. Gladstone's enthusiasm for Irish Home Rule split his Liberal party in 1886 but plenty of Scottish Liberals were enthusiastic about Home Rule for Scotland. The Liberals were unquestionably the dominant political party of the day in Scotland. The Conservatives' opposition to parliamentary reform and their identification with the despised church patronage which had led to the Disruption in 1843 had already condemned them to second place in the political allegiance of the Scots.

The Twentieth Century: Two World Wars and the Birth of the SNP

What use to let a sunrise fade
To ha'e anither like't the morn
Or let a generation pass
That ane nae better may succeed
Or wi' a' Time's machinery
Keep naething new aneth the sun
Or change things oot o' kennin' that
They may be mair the same?

A Drunk Man Looks at the Thistle, Hugh MacDiarmid

The Liberals were back in power by 1906 with Home Rule once more on their agenda. Asquith steered Home Rule for Ireland through the Commons but it was suspended because of the outbreak of World War 1. The equivalent legislation for Scotland, though it had reached its second reading in the House of Commons, also fell victim to the disruption caused by the war. Support for Scottish Home Rule before the war was buoyed up by an economic confidence which derived from massive industrial output. Scotland's shipbuilding production, which had benefited significantly from the tension caused by German expansionism, was greater than that of either Germany or America in 1913. However, after the war, prospects for Scotland's heavy industry and other key parts of her economy did not look so bright. Pre-war exports of heavy machinery had merely served to provide Scotland's international rivals with an excellent basis for winning trade from Scotland herself. For example, the new jute industry in India which relied on machinery imported from Scotland was very much responsible for the decline in Dundee's position as a major textile exporter. After the war, moreover, oil was replacing coal as the most competitive fuel and Scotland had to rely on coal.

Post-war Scotland's economic problems seemed more acute than those of England and Home Rule returned to the agenda. Now, however, the main anti-Unionist party was the Labour Party. Nationalism and the politics of class conflict had started off as uneasy bed-fellows in the Scottish Parliamentary Labour Party. Its MPs came up against another problem which would become a familiar part of the tangled history of parliamentary campaigns for increased Scottish political autonomy: the frustration of the radical Scots voice finding itself consistently stifled at Westminster by the votes of English Labour members. As the radical Jimmie Maxton complained, they were 'pledged to a policy of social stagnation'. This explains the fate of Labour's Home Rule Bills of 1924 and 1927. Both of these were doomed by general parliamentary indifference to the project of Scottish Home Rule. The next decade began with a slump of unprecedented severity and the resulting need for centralist intervention completely eclipsed Home Rule aspirations in the Labour movement.

As a response to Labour's failure to deliver Home Rule, the early 1930s saw the birth of the Scottish National Party. At this point, it was a tiny sect of middle-class intellectuals including Hugh MacDiarmid, Neil Gunn and Compton MacKenzie. The 1939-1945 war inspired fierce factional debate within the SNP about whether or not its members should contribute to the British war effort. In contrast, the Labour Party, under Tom Johnstone, the Scottish Secretary of State in Churchill's wartime Government, showed what valuable reforms, like the Hydro-Electric Board, could be effected in Scotland without any reference to Home Rule which Johnstone called 'an irrelevance'.

Throughout the rest of the 1940s and 1950s Labour's pre-eminence in Scottish politics concentrated on interventionist economics rather than Home Rule. The party pursued the policies of class struggle within the Union setting, condemning the SNP as 'Tartan Tories'. Meanwhile the Conservative Party remained as committed as ever to the Union and, like Labour, intervened when in power at Westminster to boost the Scottish economy by importing industrial projects from the south.

The interventionist records of the two parties include the following:

Labour	Invergordon Aluminium Smelter
	Dounreay Nuclear Power Station
	Highlands and Islands Development Board
Tories	Linwood and Bathgate car assembly plants
	Ravenscraig Steel Works

That none of these enterprises still exists must say something about the way economic intervention in Scotland was managed by both parties and calls into question the wisdom of transplanting industrial development on to the Scots economy from outside.

By the 1960s, it was clear that the Labour Party had abandoned Home Rule despite repeated attempts by Party activists to have it reinstated as official policy. This, combined with the trend towards the centralist control of Harold Wilson's governments, caused a decline in Labour's Scottish support. After the high point of their 55% share of the vote in 1955, the Conservative Party experienced a permanent decline in credibility among Scottish voters. As the memory of the British victory of 1945 and the glamour of the British Empire faded, the SNP began to attract increased support from a wider social grouping than previously. Organisation improved and by-election votes increased accordingly. Their first by-election win came at Hamilton in 1967. Although the victor, Winnie Ewing, lost her seat in the General

Election two years later, her victory combined with impressive SNP performances in local government elections to cause both Unionist parties significant alarm.

The history of both main parties' interest in reform of the Union during the next decade was very much as a tactic for deflating the electoral threat of the SNP. The Labour Party feared greatly for its near-monopoly of the Scots working-class vote and both parties were loath to endanger Westminster's control of Scotland once the development of the Scottish oil fields had begun in the mid-1970s. While the practical consequences of Unionist-sponsored Devolution were always problematic, one of its chief purposes was to remove the *raison d'être* of the SNP. The possibility of Devolution certainly did exacerbate the internal division in the SNP over tactics for achieving Scottish political autonomy. During the 1970s the Tories under Edward Heath and then the Labour Party under Harold Wilson and Jim Callaghan continued the charade of supporting Devolution. No doubt there were genuine pro-Devolutionists at Westminster but it must be remembered that it was Jim Callaghan's minority government's parliamentary dependence on the SNP which ultimately inspired his Devolution Referendum rather than any deep-seated belief in Home Rule. The failure of the eventual 1979 Referendum on Devolution had, therefore, more to do with the less than total commitment of the Labour Party to Devolution than any failure of nerve by the Scots voters. For one thing the Labour Party was openly split on the issue, not a very inspiring message to the voters of Scotland. Worse still, the weakness of Callaghan's position meant he had to allow George Cunningham's crucial Labour amendment, making the results of a pro-Devolution decision binding only if 40% or more Scots votes were so cast. This meant that the fairly narrow margin of the 1.23 million voting in favour of Devolution over 1.15 million voting against it was insufficient to ensure Devolution as only 32.9% of the electorate had voted for Devolution.

There were other party political reasons for the result of the Devolution Referendum. The economy was in a bad way and the result of the Referendum may have been in part a result of Callaghan's failure to govern Britain effectively. The SNP lost little time in exploiting this weakness. They withdrew their parliamentary support from the Labour Government after the failure of the Referendum. Their Motion of Censure led directly to the 1979 General Election and the Premiership of Margaret Thatcher. David Steel, as he joined with the SNP to pull the rug from under Jim Callaghan, felt confident that it was only a matter of time before a successful Devolution Referendum would be held. I do not envy him his eighteen years of discovering how wrong he was.

From Thatcher to Now

That dreadful, dreadful woman

At the start of the 1980s there was only mass disillusionment with the whole Devolution issue. Then Thatcherism began to bite. When Margaret Thatcher first became leader of the Tories in 1975 she promised her party 'a better Devolution Bill', but by the time she arrived at Downing Street she had lost interest in constitutional reform. The Falklands War gave her the opportunity to be as sickening a British patriot as could be imagined. Throughout the Thatcher years, Scotland voted decisively for Labour and continued to be served up the same monetarist ideology which increasingly seemed to be dissolving the very fabric of life in Scotland especially what made it different from (particularly the south-east of) England. For examples of this difference endangered by Thatcherite assaults on the Scots way of life, all we need to mention is the undermining of Scottish educational provision, the sale and running-down of council house stock and the various privatisations demanded by monetarist dogma. A symbolic snapshot of the glaring mismatch between Margaret Thatcher and Scots consciousness came in May 1988 when she addressed the General Assembly of the Church of Scotland, having apparently invited herself to do so. The tactless ignorance she displayed on this occasion was shocking but inevitably not surprising. The contrast between the Prime Minister and her audience epitomised the gulf between her and the Scottish Kirk as expressions of particular English and Scots world views.

The idea that the Tories tried out the Poll Tax on Scotland first is a tempting explanation for that bodged reform of local government finance attempted by Margaret Thatcher's Government in 1985. In fact it was the tiny handful of Scottish Tory MPs who rushed her new legislation into action in Scotland to save their own electoral skins. A revaluation of rateable property that was due in Scotland which meant that some people (in Tory constituencies) might have had to pay greatly increased rates. The holders of these seats, tiny blue islands in a sea of anti-Thatcher voters, pushed the implementation of the new Community Charge forward to avoid exposing themselves to rejection from their own supporters angered by huge rates bills. But whatever the motives behind its early introduction in Scotland, the blatant flaws in the Poll Tax legislation made a huge contribution to the development of a new sort of resistance to the late-20th century version of English heavy-handedness in Scotland. The other parliamentary parties had proved unable to keep the Tories from dominating a whole decade in Scottish politics without even the ghost of a mandate. It was, therefore, time for another sort of politics, one which would transcend the century-old stalemate of parliamentary attempts to wrest at least some political power from Westminster.

The Campaign for a Scottish Assembly had been founded in the aftermath of the 1979 Referendum and turned out to be a cross-party amalgam working for change in the constitutional arrangements of the Union. It was the CSA mixture of chiefly Labour, Trades Union and SNP personnel which eventually launched the Scottish Constitutional Convention in 1988, after the Labour majority in Scotland had been forced to witness Margaret Thatcher's third General Election victory. Labour and the SNP suspended their mutual distaste for a while and the STUC, the Liberal/SDP, the Scottish Greens and a range of Scottish church representatives also took part in the SCC. The SNP's involvement did not in fact survive the effect of an SNP by-election victory in late 1988. This signalled to the SNP, as did complaints from their grassroots supporters about their hob-nobbing with Labour, that they did not automatically stand to gain from participation in the Convention. Purely pro-Independence politics do, after all, stand to be seriously compromised by Devolution. The Convention proceeded without the SNP, putting together an array of innovative ideas about how Scotland could be more satisfactorily run from Scotland. This contributed to a build-up amongst Scots nationwide of a sense that the next General Election would lead to lasting and significant changes. It actually became cool to support the SNP; Rupert Murdoch realised this and sanctioned the Scottish Sun's pro-Independence line. Ravenscraig, one of the last major heavy industry producers in Scotland, was closed at the beginning of January 1992 with the Westminster government apparently unable or unwilling to save it. Just before the General Election later in the same year, John Major, pallid successor to Margaret Thatcher, came to Scotland to argue passionately for the Union. He promised to 'take stock' of Scotland's situation after a Conservative election victory. Not many felt this to be a likely outcome, either the stock-take or a Conservative fourth term: the success of coalition grassroots politics had vastly increased Scotland's sense of the politically possible.

The result, therefore, was the ultimate scunner probably because pre-election confidence was at least partly based on unfounded over-enthusiasm from those politicians and journalists whose job it was to emphasise the strength of anti-Unionist chances. The fact that the Tory vote went up may well be explained by this hype having brought out voters to defend the Union. Yet despite the efforts made by the Tories to mobilise their supporters, the Union still fared badly: fifty-eight out of seventy-two Scots MPs were elected on a Home Rule platform. John Major did institute the near-meaningless concession of the Scottish Grand Committee but little else was done in the way of stock-taking. In a speech after the election, John Major admitted the strategic importance of the Union as a foundation for Britain's international prestige; Scottish self-government would be bound to reduce Britain's influence in Europe and the world. What, of course, he really meant was that alone England would not count internationally for as much as Scotland and England together.

So, the Scots have been voting for an increased control of their own affairs for over a century. They have been encouraged and then disappointed by a parade of politicians: Herbert Asquith, Ramsay MacDonald, Winston Churchill, Alec Douglas-Home, Edward Heath, Harold Wilson, Jim Callaghan, Margaret Thatcher, Neil Kinnock – and Tony Blair? Nineteen Parliamentary Bills have attempted to legislate for Scottish Home Rule, but as we have seen, both Conservative and Labour leaderships have so far only been interested in Scotland's constitutional future for their own tactical reasons. Once safely in power, they invoke the procedural inertia of the *status quo* to preserve the Union of 1707. Tony Blair cannot be accused of such desertion but the effective practical outcome of his Devolution policy must be the ultimate test of his good intentions.

Signs

How should I conclude this chronology? When I began work on it, the shock Conservative victory of 1992 and the accumulated weight of nearly two decades of Tory rule made it strangely difficult for me to imagine the possibility of real change. The previous nine hundred years had seen Scottish suffering, directly or indirectly, at England's hands, perpetuated by physical and material force, then by Imperial hegemony and finally parliamentary inertia. After all this time could England really relinquish her dominant, domineering position? The May 1997 election result certainly broke the spell of eternal Tory control. The last five years of Tory rule featuring weak leadership, violent public disagreements over Europe and loads of sleaze produced a correspondingly extreme reaction. New Labour, party of Devolution, won a fabulous majority. Moreover, Tory refusal even to countenance Devolution in Scotland and Wales only earned their party parliamentary annihilation in both countries.

However, even such a decisive victory leaves plenty of question marks about how Devolution is achieved and how it is made to work in practice. Tony Blair, at the time of writing, still looks every inch the reforming, modernising *wonderkind* Prime Minister: stunning bone structure and a decisive majority to match. By the time what I am writing has been published, a Devolution Referendum and the subsequent establishment of a Scottish Parliament could have all gone ahead without a hiccough. But as I write, many issues still exist which might keep the Auld Sang of Scottish resentment of England alive a while longer. Many people feel, for example, that Blair has not properly addressed the question of whether or not it is fair for Scottish MPs to debate English issues at Westminster if English MPs no longer have a say in Scottish affairs. Blair has failed to supply a clear-cut answer to this question. As if to indicate a lurking uncertainty at odds with his stated intention to achieve Devolution, there were quite a few wobbly moments in the election campaign itself, especially when Blair came back to the land of his birth. He claimed afterwards that he hadn't meant, 'Sovereignty resides in me as an English MP,' which he said in an interview with *The Scotsman*. But like the two-question Referendum it made me wonder about his real intention. Of course, when you read this such doubts may have been proved wrong. Historically though, Labour's record on Devolution is not reassuring.

However, even Devolution Labour-style may not signal the end of justified Scottish resentment of England. There is a new generation of Scots since the failure of the last attempt to secure Devolution which has grown up in the full glare of the bad publicity provoked by the democratic and economic iniquities of the Union. This generation is far less constrained than previous ones by any automatic deference to Westminster, the Royal Family, the BBC and London-as-the-Centre-of-the Universe. Rather, they can draw their inspiration from the history and culture(s) of their own country. Traditional Scottish music and dance are enjoyed by all sorts of young people today. *Braveheart, Rob Roy* and *Trainspotting* may not have been totally representative of a real Scotland, but they rely wholly on vibrant notions of Scotland. These very successful films could not possibly have been set anywhere else. This post '79 generation believes far more powerfully in Scottish possibilities than any before them. This may mean, ultimately, they are more likely to be critical of any Devolution package which doesn't deliver in ways they perceive as worthwhile. In February 1997, *The Times* published an opinion poll which suggested that 50% of Britons believed that Scottish Devolution would lead inevitably to Scottish Independence. Such an outcome might certainly result if Scottish self-confidence was to be disappointed and frustrated by incomplete or inadequate Devolution provisions.

It's not just the radical and young who may have serious reasons to be critical of constitutional changes which don't go far enough. The Union remains essentially undemocratic despite the Tories' nemesis. Some have derived a savage satisfaction from seeing the end of the Tory control of Scotland which had no democratic basis. But in the same way as the Tory domination was somehow wrong, the complete absence of Tory MPs in Scotland is also wrong as 25% of Scots voted Conservative in the '97 election. The relationship between England and Scotland and between the two countries' political components is surely too subtle to be properly expressed by the blunt instrument of the first-past-the-post electoral system. 25% is too large a slice of the population to be sidelined in this way, however pleasing a spectacle is provided by former Tory MPs' miracle conversion to all sorts of previously undreamed of notions, such as PR and standing for election to a Scottish Parliament.

Last but not least of the possible flash-points which might seriously disrupt the brave new world of Labour-sponsored Devolution is the undeniable fact that to control the all-important Westminster Parliament (which is going to stay all-powerful despite Labour's claims about the importance of their Scottish Assembly), the British Labour Party needs the Scottish Labour Party. Any development which might lead ultimately to a Parliamentary Labour Party made up only of English members could leave the Westminster PLP fatally weakened. Looking for an understanding of the significant differences between England and Scotland is one part of the quest I embarked on when I first discovered, on arrival here ten years ago, that the two countries are not simply interchangeable parts of a homogeneous territory. History provided a sound, worthwhile alternative explanation of these differences and the 1997 election emphasises a crucial difference in terms of surviving Tory MPs. England still has one hundred and sixty-five: Scotland does not have any.

Therefore, as the events of 1997 have shown, it is difficult to finish a chronology while 'the dollar', as they say in Norfolk, 'is still dancing'. And as far as Scottish Devolution is concerned, there is still plenty to be resolved. Accordingly, I decided that the best way to finish off this chronology would be to take an up-to-date look at Scotland's strengths and see how far we have come in one thousand years from the small, poverty-stricken and divided (in more ways than one) country of Malcolm Canmore. My historical survey was intended to demonstrate that the historical relationship between England and Scotland was, from the very start of their history as distinct countries, powerfully influenced by the geographical advantages of size and natural wealth which England always had over Scotland. These pre-industrial advantages were decisive enough to shape events well into the 20th century. However, now the British Empire has risen and more or less fallen and hitherto unimaginable technologies and commodities dominate our lives, personally and politically. England is still physically bigger than Scotland and has a greater population. But a resultant all-round superiority can no longer be assumed. In many ways Scotland appears to be heading into the 21st century with some impressive built-in assets of her own.

There is even scope to reassess many of Scotland's original disadvantages. The relative shortage of cultivable land is now almost insignificant given the current ease of importing food from all round the world. The crucial difficulties in pre-industrial communications have been largely overcome by a fairly comprehensive development of roads and bridges plus the establishment of rail, ferry and aeroplane services. Telecommunications have advanced in seemingly miraculous ways and can now overcome many of the obstacles previously presented by Scotland's difficult terrain. An emblem of the advantages these new technologies have brought to the Highlands is the new University of the Highlands and Islands which will depend almost exclusively on electronic communications to deliver teaching to its undergraduates at sites all over the Highlands and Islands.

Highland residents can still make plenty of justifiable criticisms of rail and road provisions and the constant irritation of highly priced motor fuel north of the Central Belt has still to be satisfactorily dealt with by the petrol companies. But the Highlands is no longer that remote destination to which Dr Johnson and his friend, Boswell, travelled almost in the manner of inter-continental explorers. Moreover, *Silicon Glen* in the Central Belt continues to attract international companies keen to set up production using the proven high productivity and skill levels which exist there. No great consolation for the unemployed steelworkers and miners of that area but Scotland's role as a leading manufacturer of modern communications equipment is assured.

There have been few such radical changes to the natural environment of northern Scotland or to parts of central and southern Scotland either. In the Highlands, intensive agriculture is limited to the east coast, heavy industry which is largely confined to oil rig fabrication and servicing also takes place on the east coast. The Highland air is clean and so is much of the coastline, particularly in the west. Unlike England, Scotland has no shortage of clean, fresh water. Massive scope exists for the commercial development of wind and wave power which could combine with existing hydro-electric schemes to make Scotland a net exporter of energy produced from renewable resources. As for energy produced using non-renewable resources, Scotland's potential oil wealth constitutes a crucial built-in asset in a world economy still very much dominated by petrochemical technology. In an economic and environmental evaluation of Scotland's political options, published by the Edinburgh University's Centre for Human Ecology in 1995,

Malcolm Slesser and David Cooper Crane calculated that full ownership of her own physical resources would make 'Scotland's balance of international payments... in relative terms, highly positive'. Scotland's other potentially productive resources include coal, fish, forestry and enough clean coastline to provide the sites for more extensive fish and shellfish culture than exists at present. Slesser and Crane conclude their study in the following significant way:

> Everyone has their own view of how Scotland should and could be governed. Public opinion polls show that should and could are not the same thing. Some fear for their pensions, others that industry will flee. We choose not to enter this realm of the debate, which is best left to the politicians. What is clear is that from an economic point of view there is no reason why an independent Scotland should not prosper if properly governed. There is the potential for a higher material standard of living and more jobs. Equally, Scotland today is not really any more disadvantaged than much of the rest of the UK. In the end we suspect that many of the arguments between status quo and self-government will hinge on quality of life and the right to make one's own decisions. The economic argument is seen to be sterile and irrelevant. Scotland could stand on its own well enough, but with each passing barrel of oil that valuable initial impetus of a surplus will be diminished.

So much for the countables. Yet, the sum of a country's potential must exceed its purely material assets. There is a continuum of Scottish resources which runs from the concrete to the abstract. The Scottish, particularly the Highland, landscape is situated somewhere near the mid-point of this continuum: you can't quantify views or value natural features but money earned from the tourists which come to Scotland to see them is a major countable element in the Scottish economy, standing at £2428m for 1996. Scotland offers a unique chance to experience the last great European wilderness.

So far, in this chronology's concluding section, I have not dwelt on direct comparisons of Scotland and England, but at the abstract end of Scotland's asset list, such comparisons are too telling to resist. Tourism is only one aspect of Scotland's relationship with the rest of the world. For much of the last thousand years, Scotland has enjoyed a significantly more constructive relationship with Europe than has England. The Auld Alliance with France featured not just territorial considerations but a sizeable volume of trade. Holland also had extensive commercial relations with Scotland and was the destination for generations of Scottish travellers and students. Scotland, particularly the north-east, had strong trading links with the Baltic region and many Scots professionals and artisans found employment in Scandinavia as well as Russia up to 1917.

The SNP's idea of Independence in Europe is, therefore, more than a convenient *ad hoc* ploy. Not only does Scotland's relationship with Europe have some historical foundations but there is an up-to-date congruence between the municipalism of much Scottish life and the Centralist/Socialist intentions of the European Community, as apparent, for example, in the Social Chapter. The Conservative Government specifically rejected this element of European legislation, and although its Labour successors always supported the Social Chapter, there is a fault-line of deep ambivalence about Europe running through all of the English establishment. It is ironic to note that much of this ambivalence is concerned with ideas about national sovereignty, and this from a parliamentary system which has taken over a century properly to address the question of Scottish Home Rule. Not all Scots are pro-Europeans but there is undoubtedly a significant Scottish tradition of engagement with Europe.

There are plenty of Scots who reject tartanry in all its forms and no doubt Scottish anarchists exist who wouldn't thank you for a Scottish nation state if they were offered it. But as I've said elsewhere in this book, more Scots seem to enjoy a belief in the idea of Scotland than the English do about their own country. Scottish traditional culture, in all its various, more or less authentic, forms, has strong grass roots adherence in a way which has no equivalent in England. There, a somewhat touristy cosmopolitanism and a mix of embarrassment about, and pride in the Empire is what is more apparent. English national sentiment tends in the main to be the business of Conservative nostalgia merchants at best and the British Union of Fascists at worst. There is a terrific cynicism about the strength of English political life and the country's ability successfully to manage decline, let alone reverse it. Effective, constructive patriotism seems to be missing from England and many of her people. There are, for instance, among the hordes of English-born living in the Highlands no formal or informal English associations. It's hard to imagine a single radio/television station based even partly on English culture and history. Radio Scotland, with its intelligent and non-ironic coverage of Scottish historical and cultural matters has no obvious counterpart in England: Radio 4 is *British* Radio 4, most definitely not *Radio England* despite its often irritating Anglo-centricity.

This sense of commitment to the idea of Scotland leads me to the final Scottish asset in my list. While apparently a part of the country's uncountable assets, it could be a factor which could have practical effects in the relative developments of the two countries. I refer here to the way Scotland's greater sense of pride and belief in itself is mediated through Scottish society. In Scotland there is a far greater sense of community and civil society than has survived in England, especially after Margaret Thatcher. This claim is, of course, impossible to substantiate with figures but I was struck by some major differences between Scotland and England as soon as I came to live in the Highlands. As I noted earlier, the pages of local newspapers were full of accounts of, and advertisements for, community-based and small-scale activities from business news and local government news through various religious groups, to a myriad of cultural activities. My initial impression of genuine grass roots vibrancy has only strengthened in the ten years I have been in the Highlands. I've seen plenty more evidence that it is a Scotland-wide phenomenon. My own experience of these community-scale activities confirms my initial feeling that unlike most English equivalents they are not wholly a middle-class preserve. This is very much a reflection of an important aspect of Scots' feelings about Scotland. Scottish patriotism is available for all classes in all political persuasions and the paraphernalia of Scottish patriotism exists differently for all social classes. There is the kitsch of Nessie tea-towels, the bourgeois respectability of full Highland dress for many Scottish weddings and the more patrician balls and meetings patronised by the landed and wealthy and their associates. All are expressions of a pride in Scotland, even if that Scotland might mean different things to different people.

A Highland Games provides an excellent chance to see this principle in action. There will be lairds among the farmers showing livestock, middle-class matrons preside over the SWRI's exhibition of cooking and crafts and the sporting competitions come from all classes. But the beer tent is everybody's and the catering arrangements are strictly single-tier. The Highland dancers wear fancy tartan outfits of dubious historical origin but display an athletic grace which is generally admired. It must be a costly arena to enter but it seems that people from all backgrounds encourage their children to participate. To complete this microcosmic representation of Scotland, there are always plenty of tourists in attendance, whatever the weather. Yet the Games are a quintessentially Scottish affair. They are proud to feature activities and characteristics which are considered to be traditionally Scottish and it is this perception rather than actual authenticity which matters. So, what significance does this picturesque tableau have in an audit of Scotland's present-day strengths? More than a few of the English incomers that I interviewed commented on Scotland's classlessness; at least in comparison to England. Even if the Scots' claim to be 'all Jock Tamson's bairns' does not completely reflect reality, it seems that if Scots do classify their neighbours, they are more likely to do so on the basis of achievements rather than any inherited wealth or social position, as is still often the case in England. Such egalitarianism must contribute decisively to the cohesiveness of civil society and strengthen the underpinnings of community. Indeed, community does seem to be more practically in evidence north of the border, in rural areas as well as towns and cities. (I have described my own experiences of this already.) Strength of community is not a countable either, yet I can't help thinking it must promote significant tangible advantages for Scotland.

There is one last item to add to the list of Scotland's current strengths. It is another intangible connected to well-developed notions of community but comes, in fact, definitely at the concrete end of the continuum. Scotland is a small country with a population roughly half that of London. This fact works to reinforce a sense of community and shared experience at a national level. I can well believe the often-quoted notion that two Scots strangers travelling in the same train from Edinburgh to Kings Cross are bound to have discovered mutual connections before the end of the journey. I have, *via* Scots friends, experienced versions of this myself on several occasions. Scots enjoy a comparable geographical familiarity with their country too: more places than just the obvious beauty spots are well-known and loved in a shared way. Population size, is of course, a countable but can the effects of a relatively small population really make any telling contribution to a country's strength? Surely, more people equals more power? It certainly did in the 13th century. Yet, I would argue that there is a strength in this inter-connectedness of people and country which could produce in the 21st century a power just as significant as that deriving from mere numbers. Scots are patently not homogeneous, socially or politically, but they share many, many relationships and experiences.

Perhaps the Scots' most powerful shared possession is a body of approximately common moral perceptions. An example I can cite to support such an assertion is the way Scotland generally resisted Thatcherism in most of its aspects as far as it was able. A significant instance of this resistance came in the mid-'80s when the Scottish teaching union, the EIS, got massive support from parents for the industrial action it took against Tory educational policies and their threatened anglicisation of the Scots system. Historically, the English have seen much to admire in Scottish education. Perhaps this admiration is ultimately inspired by an unmistakable Scots belief in the importance of education for individuals and society alike: that is not just education *per se* but education of a specific moral purpose. As Dr Archie Watt, Moderator of the Church of Scotland warned in 1966,

> ...don't become concerned with the material advantages of education and lose sight of the quality of the men and women our schools and colleges produce.
>
> Should the light of their minds be made artificial by the fake promises of an irresponsible affluence and distorted into a ruthless rat race for self-aggrandisement, then we shall be producing a generation which may be clever but not cultured, and a leadership which is neither educated in the best sence of the term, nor responsible.
>
> quoted by Hugh MacDiarmid in *The Company I've Kept*, 1966

NOTES FROM THE NORTH

The comparisons in this conclusion do not turn the tables on England, the bigger, stronger country. It is still a rich and populous place. But as the millennium approaches, Scotland has certain assets which may well make decisive contributions to her flourishing in the 21st century.

CHAPTER 4

A short step south;
Questions and Answers

AFTER TWO YEARS IN SUTHERLAND I had to admit my wonderful new life wasn't really working out. I would never have enough of the views from my steading or tire of the company of the folk who were my neighbours, incomers and natives alike. But unlike many of the English in that part of Sutherland, I had not gone there to retire. All the casual work available in the area like tree-planting, deer stalking and farm work wasn't quite compatible with looking after a toddler and I'd failed to find anybody interested in making mutual childcare arrangements. So it appeared I was not properly qualified to make a living in Sutherland and I had begun to realise that living in the empty, remote Highlands did not nowadays entail the same sort of frugal subsistence that had, perforce, been practised there by earlier generations. I was irrevocably tied to the demands of the modern cash economy. For one thing, I needed a reliable car which would not grind to a halt on a lonely road (few roads in Sutherland are anything else) or fail to start when I had to fetch vital supplies. Heating can be quite expensive 300 feet above sea-level and only 1,200 miles (less than the distance to Paris) from the Arctic Ocean. I wasn't trying to survive in a desert but there was definitely less margin of error than in more convenient, less spectacular places. Yet it was not just pride which stopped me from considering going back to England for good. I was hooked: I had revelled in the Highlands where, as Robert Louis Stevenson wrote, 'essential silence chills and blesses'.

I simply could not entertain the prospect of returning to stuffy, fenced-off Norfolk. An English woman, resident in the Highlands for over twenty years, whom I'd met through my English neighbours told me about a house to rent near a small town in Easter Ross. The county of Ross-shire, due south of Sutherland, spans northern Scotland coast-to-coast but most of its population is concentrated in the fertile strip of Easter Ross which lies between the North Sea coast and the big hills which march all the way over to the west, their solitude broken only by occasional tiny settlements. Easter Ross, while nothing like as busy as most of England, has a much higher population density than Sutherland or Wester Ross. I decided this was necessary for the purposes of earning a few more quid as well as for the sake of my daughter who hadn't met many other children in her short life. The 'essential silence' had been gorgeous, but now there were two of us with concrete requirements which only a wider community could fulfil.

I did earn more money in Ross-shire and my daughter did get to go to a playgroup. Suddenly, I had a social life and could pop into the supermarket every day if I wanted; the nearest one had been over twenty miles away in Sutherland. But it was as if the need to take responsibility for myself and my child had exposed my Sutherland idyll as nothing more heroic than glorified tourism. I hadn't been able to sustain employment by engaging successfully with the local economy so the reality of my life there was no more substantial than an idea: the idea of living in a beautiful, empty place for no better reason than that it was a beautiful, empty place. Easter Ross showed up further contradictions in the whole project of transplanting myself to a better place.

The first thing I discovered there was that moving north from England did not ensure a complete escape from environmental degradation. I had only travelled forty miles south from the steading with its curlews, wild flowers and vista of endless hilltops but I had returned to substantially the same world of agribusiness I had sought to leave behind me. A few more wildflowers survived than there were in Norfolk and the fields weren't quite so huge as the East Anglian prairies but the Cromarty Firth which my new home overlooked is significantly if not visibly polluted by the run-off into it of agricultural chemicals, by the oil rig fabrication and servicing industries which exist on its shores and by the sewage pumped into it daily from the coastal towns. Wherever you go, there's no real possibility of escaping from the mess human beings make once they get busy.

My presence in the Highlands was also called into question in another way in Easter Ross: by the people there. As the oil rig fabrication boom of the early 1980s had contracted, more and more working people were having to go further away from home to find work that was better paid than any of the useless old jokes offered by the tourism industry. When I talked with the other women at the playgroup about how I'd come to the Highlands for the quality of life, I sensed that they weren't especially interested. I began to realise that they were probably more concerned with how far away their men would have to go to earn enough to pay the mortgage. And, of course, at the back of that anxiety lurked the possibility of the oldest Highland tradition of all: clearing out, changing places, or countries, or even continents, simply to survive economically. Fortunately, down in the sandpit, the under-fives didn't care if my daughter was English or Scots but some of the grown ups didn't find it so easy to turn the other cheek. It was in Easter Ross that I understood a little of what it must be like to be judged and found wanting according to the relatively accidental factor of birth place or skin colour.

You've seen how I feel about community. Going to Easter Ross, I supposed I would find it easier to find and experience community. More populous but not overcrowded, this, surely, would be the place where I could find something of those human relationships for which I'd been longing all those years in England: settlements small enough for everyone to know something of many of his or her neighbours. Anonymity amongst people would be replaced by connectedness, mutual support, shared experiences: ceilidh land! That's certainly what I was hoping for, but my experience of Easter Ross showed up the fatal flaws in my assumptions that the benefits of Highland community life could be enjoyed as easily as one might slip on an old overcoat. Looking back, I sense the same inevitability about this disappointment just like studying the history of the Highlands exposed my revelling in the emptiness of the glens and straths as ignorant and insensitive in the extreme.

The very strength of this little community where I had come to live meant that, unless you were someone special in a particularly useful way like a nurse, doctor, teacher or a major employer, it didn't actually need you. As my experience at the sandpit had shown, this group of people, tied by kinship and generations of close proximity, had no need of or reference point for irrelevant strangers who had chosen to define its arena of daily struggle as a relaxing backwater.

But through work and the fact of having a child (a wonderful reason for talking to people) I did make some good friends in Easter Ross. They included native Highlanders, incomers from all over Scotland and, inevitably, other people who had come north from England. I didn't belong to the area as the native Highlanders did but eventually I felt I was part of something in a way that had most definitely not been the case in England or Sutherland.

And what was the job that I was able to earn most from? Giving private English lessons.

Many families have had to accept that the Highlands cannot

provide their children with a wide range of employment opportunities. They realise that education is their children's best chance of an escape ticket to brighter economic prospects. For most, this means Higher Education and in Scotland, to study nearly everything from medicine to hotel management, students first have to obtain a pass in Higher English (a Higher is roughly equivalent to England's 'A' level, but in Scotland more subjects are usually studied over one year per Higher rather than two). It is, therefore, critical for students hoping to gain university or college admission to pass Higher English. So, the main contribution I could make to this determined, self-confident community was to aid and abet those wanting to help their children leave it *via* the education system. This irony and my former aversion to private education make a strange comment on how I was prepared to support myself in the country which from England had seemed like the promised land deserving of my best behaviour.

Easter Ross was busier than Sutherland which meant a greater chance of anonymity for its inhabitants. This left room for more noticeable anti-English feeling than I had experienced in Sutherland. Nothing physical, nothing frightening, nothing worse than a general sense of native irritation with the ubiquitous English which one learnt about through Highland friends who, naturally, claimed not to share such prejudices. This irritation had been growing since the serious rise in English-born incomers began in c.1970.

	1971	1981	1991
Total Population	163,873	187,004	204,004
Number born in England	10,785	17,079	24,255
Percentage born in England	6.6%	9.1%	11.9%

Based on Highland Region Census Extracts

I wanted to canvass Highland opinion on the subjects of place and belonging. I only received one letter which was written in confidence and focused on English incomers.

> Their involvement in Councils and committees and social groups mean the traditional reserved Highlander now feels squeezed out of his own environment. The ultimate loser is of course the incoming English people. It is sad that their energetic resolve to improve, pioneer and become involved is destroying the very thing they have come to find [remembers his village before any English had arrived] now today I would guess they and other incomers (Scots and others) outnumber the locals considerably and the harmony and peace of C___ is gone. I have never known disagreement, isolation and petty squabbling as now exists and this applies elsewhere.

You didn't need ESP to pick up the fact that England was seen as the origin of much trouble and disappointment for Highlanders, past and present. Margaret Thatcher's replacement by John Major could not be expected seriously to diminish this perception. And there were always plenty of English individuals who seemed fated to fulfil stereotypically negative expectations, from the high profile wrong 'uns like Keith Schellenberg who treated his tenants on Eigg with such open disdain, to individuals you overheard in supermarkets declaiming their preferences loudly to one another in a most un-Highland fashion. There were plenty of others about whom it would be misleading and unfair to generalise. But the ones who received all the publicity for behaviour so disrespectful to the indigenous population were the ones who seemed all of a piece with the thousand-year parade of high-handed contempt originating in England.

The following is from a chapter entitled *The Highland Problem* in *Spade among the Rushes* by Margaret Leigh, an Englishwoman who settled on the west coast of the Highlands in the late 1940s:

But he [the Highlander] rarely takes any practical steps to get what he wants by his own exertions, or to improve what he already has: this can be seen in many places and in many things, large and small. Away from home, away from the enervating and unpredictable climate, and away from the slow rhythm of traditional life he would be different just as his kinsmen overseas are different... [and in the] bad old days by necessity his fathers were different for otherwise they could not have survived. If too little was given then, too much is given now - too much and of the wrong sort in the wrong way. And it seems likely that emigration, whether overseas or to the towns has drained the Highlands of the best and most enterprising, so that the home population, whether it likes it or no, can only breed from weaker stock.

I was now overpoweringly aware of the many contexts in which English meant trouble. I had looked hard at the tangles between Scotland and England in the previous millennium or so. There was, of course, no trace of a conscious long-term English conspiracy against the Scots. Rather, each of the more or less grisly interactions between the two countries shows England and her representatives responding to major political, economic or historical developments with her own interests very much in mind. Scotland, including and especially the Highlands, is consistently made vulnerable to these developments by material poverty and difficulties in external and internal communications. Perhaps Scotland's most decisive misfortune was to be stuck with what would become the HQ of the mighty British Empire for a next-door neighbour. England was always made practically insecure by Scotland's ability to withstand complete conquest and England has never achieved complete domination of Scotland, not even culturally. At some point (1707 to be exact) England, the bigger sibling of my earlier image, forces the smaller one to grow up and stop causing trouble by interfering with the serious project of world-domination. The Union was not a mature settlement made between equals but the more powerful nation's attempts to achieve a secure backyard for the undertaking of its own business. Such an outcome was obtained by bribes and threats. Now, any family therapist will tell you that such highly manipulative arrangements are unlikely to work. The Union had the benefits of a spectacularly successful empire and the victorious efforts of two world wars to maintain it. It's hard to imagine any history more fortuitous for its survival. In any event, by the time I arrived in the Highlands, there was a definite sense of changed days in which the Union was coming more and more under attack in Scotland.

If 1996-1997 was remarkable for an increasingly rudderless Westminster government, the catalogue of gross insensitivities expressed by the English establishment at Scotland's expense was staggering, especially at a time when the Union's sudden loss of credibility might have suggested the need for more tactful behaviour. The Scottish beef industry could have escaped the BSE catastrophe if someone had been determined enough to point out to Europe the critical differences between Scottish and English beef husbandry. John Major's craven reliance on the Ulster Unionists in the twilight of his Premiership meant that Westminster was able to secure a special deal for Northern Ireland where beef is produced in very much the same way as it is in Scotland. The Duke of Edinburgh defended the gun lobby against Dunblane-inspired protest with hideously inappropriate analogies about golf-clubs and tennis rackets in the same week as his grandson was photographed smeared with the blood of his first Highland stag. A (now ex-) Tory MP observed, almost casually, that the bulk of 'appalling beggars' in London came from Scotland. That anonymous Westminster creature, the Audit Commission continued to dismantle by a thousand cuts the work of Scottish local government.

So disharmony between Scots and English may have its roots in the past but it was not going short of fuel as the last Tory term in office came to a close. Each time yet another incident representing this apparent lack of solidarity between the two countries made the headlines, even its neutral retailing by the BBC provoked shudders of resentment all over Scotland. The awful sense of Big Brother is screwing you was felt with all the dreary familiarity of a bruised place being clumsily injured yet again. After compiling my chronology, I find it hard to resist seeing the English incomers of the late 20th century as merely the latest episode (and perhaps the most unconsciously ironic) in the millenium chain of events which shackles England and Scotland together like the delinquent siblings of my image. How can White Settlers avoid being unwilling representatives of Big Brother England and its apparently arbitrary powers over Scotland? In Ross-shire I learnt comprehensively from friends and from less friendly people that nobody was really surprised by the White Settlers' capacity for causing trouble. That was what Scotland had come to expect from England.

The English arrivals are not, of course, part of any conscious anti-Scottish conspiracy to move themselves and often their families to a place where, for most, the answer to the question, 'Why did you come here?' is definitely not, 'For the money!' Moreover, the question, 'How did you feel once you got here?' had become increasingly pertinent for me. My own sense of not belonging in the Highlands, my gradual discovery of Scottish national aspirations (official and unofficial) had already combined with certain world events to make me aware that nationalism was not a bit ready to be consigned to the good old dustbin of history.

By 1992, the break up of Yugoslavia was irrevocably underway. Don't panic, I'm not going to attempt an analysis of the Balkan conflict. The comparison with Britain is flawed before we begin because neither Scotland nor England has any experience of some of the critical ingredients in that Balkan brew like Communist rule and tri-partite religious strife. Yet there was something about the conflict in the former Yugoslavia which added to my growing sense of unease. Since the end of World War II, Serbs, Croats and Muslims had been co-existing peacefully in a society whose modernity we could see for ourselves every night on the telly: supermarkets, motorways, cinemas and universities. Then suddenly it's all as medieval as the warlords on all sides, despite their jeeps and mobile phones.

Now, don't get me wrong. I wasn't making out a case for the White Settlers to erupt in paranoid frenzy. It's just that what happened in the former Yugoslavia seemed to suggest that if people with long-standing historical differences look like they've put the past behind them it isn't necessarily the case. Or to put it another way: the comforts of the supermarket society are no guarantee against the outbreak of violent nationalist passions. Yugoslavia provided a compelling example of the way sophisticated, apparently cosmopolitan societies can unravel into their constituent, violently opposed parts. You couldn't say for sure that such unravelling couldn't happen here. The Yugoslavian *status quo ante bellum* had been held in place by a very strong Communist state. The unravelling occurred once that state's power was fatally weakened by events in Soviet Russia and elsewhere in eastern Europe. I couldn't help wondering what would happen if a similarly fundamental change happened in Scotland – the (even temporary) collapse of the Social Security system? Or yet another Tory General Election victory? Or what if Tony Blair's pre-election wobbles and contradictions over Scotland turn out to be the tip of a huge iceberg of disappointment for Scottish aspirations. As we have seen, in Scotland such disappointments are as traditional as shortbread.

I wanted to find out what other English incomers were thinking about all this. Some, no, most of them, looked so well-established in their croft houses, craft shops, surgeries and manses that it was hard to imagine them pushing precariously-laden prams through the snow, up and down the passes of the southbound A9. Yet, I kept wondering (silently as good manners dictated) did these people ever think, 'What if?'? Did they ever regret their decision to settle in the Highlands? What did they think about the Scottish National Party and the Act of Union? Had they found whatever they had been looking for when they decided to come to the Highlands in the first place? Why had they left the country of their birth? Did they ever stop to think about any of this stuff at all? Did they mind when it stayed dark in mid-winter from 4.15pm to 9am? What did they miss about England? Would Ken and Rosemary ever bother to find out about the Battle of Carbisdale?

As I thought about all the questions that I would like to ask the English in the Highlands, I realised they would constitute an interesting enquiry into bigger issues than the personal difficulties I was having, getting used to my new *gringo* identity.

There is a Britain that likes to think of itself as a distinctly cosmopolitan society, comfortably past the stage of divisive nationalisms. Apart from Northern Ireland... Apart from the British Union of Fascists... Apart from the Sons of Owen Glendower and blazing Welsh holiday homes... Surely, the English, behind the lines in the Highlands, would provide a revealing insight into how much nationality does matter in Britain as the 20th century draws to a close. The London agenda has chosen to concentrate, however ineffectually, on defining Britain's role in Europe. Does such preoccupation take Britain's political homogeneity too much for granted?

So, inspired by the pressing contemporary relevance of these issues, I constructed a set of questions which I hoped would encourage the sort of revelations interesting for a general readership. It might also help me as I tried to make constructive sense of my new life.

These are the questions I decided to ask:

What were your reasons for coming to Scotland?
For how long were you planning the move?
What were you most looking forward to in Scotland?
What were you most pleased to be leaving behind?
What do you most miss about England now?
In what ways, if any, have your feelings about Scotland changed?
Do you consider yourself English, Scottish, British or none of these?
Describe your feelings about the Act of Union.
If you would like to see any change in the existing situation would you favour Devolution, Independence or any other change?

So, invested with the respectability of a current affairs investigator, I was going to get the chance of asking all sorts of people how they lived with the contemptuous appellation of white colonialism branded invisibly on their foreheads. I was going to get hold of some answers, answers that had been eluding me since my arrival in Scotland.

Probably it was this private agenda which made me anxious to avoid affecting the outcomes by posing questions which assumed the widespread existence of resentments on either side. I wanted to give the interviewees the option of talking about conflict rather than give them the idea that I was only interested in hearing about trouble. That turned out to be a good hunch because the denials and contradictions which I uncovered in many of my interviewees' attitudes to their new lives and to their Scots hosts might not have emerged if my questions had given them the chance to deny

outright that there was any reason to be less than content. BBC
Radio 4 came up to Inverness just as I was starting my interviews
and they *were* looking for trouble. They had heard about Settler
Watch and Scottish Watch spray-painting English-owned houses
in Aberdeen and about the public meeting a Scottish Watch group
had held in Dingwall. They were disappointed to find that nothing
much had happened. They were using interviews too. They chose
Patrick White, the publican from Inverness whose anti-English
routines had earned him public accusations of racism. They also
talked to an English woman who said moving to a village in the
Highlands was no more problematic than moving to a village in
Kent. Her Home Counties delivery was perfect for her ample sense
of self-satisfaction. They came to interview me and I fused all my
electrics trying to make them a serious, writerly cup of coffee.
During the interview I told the fabulous story about the anti-Scots
moral panic stirred up by John Wilkes in 18th century London. So
many educated Scots had come to England after 1707 to take up
jobs, especially in the burgeoning civil service, that Wilkes
achieved widespread credence for the rumour that the Scottish
Prime Minister, Lord Bute, was carrying on with the King's
mother: Scots were everywhere and taking control at the highest
level! I love this story because it shows so neatly how the power
of fear-based prejudice has operated on both sides of the border.
Naturally when the programme was broadcast they'd only got a
couple of minutes of me. Patrick White went on for hours, as well
as the Home Counties woman bullying people (politely) at an
Inverness flower show. Perhaps I should have known they
wouldn't have time for Lord Bute. But I truly did not wish to be
combative: I wanted to concentrate on how English incomers had
found ways to make accommodations with this history (side-
stepping those whose blatant tactlessness signified a lack of
interest in any sort of accommodation). At a stroke, I could trawl

people's consciences as well as conduct a revealing study of a particular interaction between two nationalities at a point in time when nationality is not supposed to be terribly important, in a place where it is rarely forgotten. I took my questionnaire, which was intended to provoke discussion as much as to obtain information, round as many different types of people as I could. I hoped to talk to an exciting range of people doing all sorts of interesting things. Coincidentally, this might provide me with a matching variety of justifications for our unbidden presence in the north of Scotland. Perhaps the solution to my discomfort was just around the corner: all I had to do was to go and tape-record it and into the bargain construct a compelling jigsaw image of English/Scottish interaction and co-existence in the Highlands.

However, despite this initial enthusiasm, a sense of deep disappointment grew as I worked through the interviews. Perhaps I had been naive or just lazy to expect other English people to have answers to the questions which powered my own *angst*. The first setback came when my hopes for a wide socio-economic range of interviewees were severely thwarted by the marked reluctance of any but the chattering (that is, middle) classes to have anything to do with the project. Some of the *refuseniks* declined politely but firmly over supermarket counters, in pubs or on buses, while the initial interest of others evaporated in missed appointments or unreturned phone calls. There were a few similar experiences at the other end of the socio-economic spectrum too. One eminent English member of the art and craft set reversed his decision to be interviewed because he wished to avoid 'promoting conflict'. In fact, rather than specify which particular conflict he had in mind he put the phone down on me in what I thought was the middle of our conversation. His was the rudest refusal I got from the smart set but not the only one.

The contradiction between claiming everything in the

Highlands is lovely and declining resolutely to discuss the subject any further even showed up in certain ways amongst those who were happy to be interviewed. There turned out to be a very disappointing rump of White Settlers who seemed to have taken advantage of the lifestyle benefits the Highlands had to offer, like space, cheap property, pure environment and (as I actually heard it expressed by one of them) enhanced leisure opportunities, without having much apparent concern for the moral implications of this change of places. I wound up with sheaves of transcripts full of the same mix of spiritual and material motives for coming to the Highlands.

'The greatest thing we got from here was the opportunity to own our own house,' appeared in numerous different versions, low property prices having proved crucial in many cases. One woman told me she and her husband had come to the Highlands because, 'Our way of life was idealistic and we reckoned we could live it here whereas we couldn't live it in other places.' Another couple spoke of coming to the Highlands as, 'The best method of getting away from it all... we chose not to work the regular paths and have a huge mortgage and if it was hard being accepted we would continue to make these choices because we reckoned we were getting a great pay-off; we were getting a lot of the things we wanted.' More than once interviewees claimed things like, 'I was led here,' or 'The Highlands are my spiritual home.' One of the '70s crop of vintage counter-culture immigrants told me he'd been welcomed to what was to become his Highland home by the local policeman assuring him, 'It's the Lord's place, it's been waiting for you.'

Yet despite this almost holy content almost every one of these enthusiasts insisted that I should preserve their anonymity in anything I might write. Implicit in their various versions of 'We found Paradise', was the claim to have achieved a problem-free integration into Highland society. It only occurred to me after a run of such interviews that there was something slightly suspect about such claims. One craft-shop owner who sounded as if she could have been speaking straight from Hemel Hempstead despite having been in the Highlands over twenty years maintained, 'I honestly don't notice whether people speak with an English or Scottish accent unless something causes me to think about it.' She and her husband were particularly keen not to be identified in print.

So my plans for a many-faceted representation of a unique inter-cultural reality, the English in the Highlands, did not work out in the straightforward go-and-get-it-and-write-it-down way I had imagined. But I did find exceptions to these complacent contradictions and they turned out to be just as interesting as exceptions are supposed to be. My egalitarian principles meant that I found having to go explicitly in search of working-class English incomers slightly embarrassing. But after six months of intermittent interviewing, the sample was still heavily weighted in favour of the middle-class. Then I met and interviewed two people, both definitely not from the comfortable classes, who had come face-to-face with a rather different Highland experience than the one about which I'd been hearing so much. One, s, had come north with her parents in the '60s following her father's engineering job. She was just about to start secondary school and she loathed Scotland at first, even taking an extra-long holiday with her grandmother in England (who didn't know about the earlier start to the Scottish academic year, fortunately for s). She came back to face the fiercely anti-English, anti-outsider atmosphere of her new school. I asked her how bad this had actually been. 'Enough to stay with you forever,' was all she would say on the subject. However, she wasn't beaten. At sixteen, she married a handsome Highland ex-serviceman and became part of his village's community. I was delighted to listen to the insights born of her dual perspective as English-born Highland wifie delivered in an apparently congenital Highland accent. (If I hadn't been told otherwise, I certainly would have assumed she was Highland born and bred.) She has seen major changes since her arrival, many connected with the advent of two non-indigenous groups. The ones she calls the 'Hi-Jimmies' are the Glaswegians brought up to the Highlands in the '60s and '70s to supply labour for the variously successful state-inspired industrial projects as well as to ease housing problems in the Central Belt. Like many native Highlanders she was cynical about the actual benefits of such social engineering which, she claimed, radically challenged the identity of her area of the Highlands. She was similarly tough on the other main group of uninvited guests to appear in large numbers in the Highlands: the English White Settlers.

Her judgements have been shaped, at least in part, by two decades of uncertain employment prospects in the Highlands: her own son and his family have been forced to travel to England to find employment suitable to his qualifications. So, she has little time for the quality of life brigade as she dubbed the English incomers. 'The quality of life is not better up here,' she insisted. 'You can't live on mountains and fresh air; you can't have a good quality of life if you're unemployed.' She has seen the Highland dream founder on these economic realities more than once. 'The English come up here for the quality of life [Oh, for punctuation marks to denote dismissive contempt in voice of speaker] after making money selling their houses. Then they can't find a way to make any more money and wind up in a council house. Moving to Scotland is just romantic nonsense. They [the English] wanted to escape the rat race and they just get into a race against nothing.'

She blamed any feelings of insecurity which English incomers might experience on their failure to get involved in local affairs. This is more common in her experience than the stereotype of the incomer tactlessly taking over everything. She is fiercely concerned for the economic fate of the Highlands and thinks the area and indeed the whole of Scotland could only benefit from Independence. She is passionately opposed to the sale of Highland estates to foreigners. 'Fair enough, come up here and live if you want to but you really have to make a contribution.'

Someone put me in touch with another working-class incomer and the story of her experience revealed very clearly just how badly things can go wrong for the English in the Highlands. As I arrived with my tape-recorder at a smartly converted croft house on the edge of one of the more notably lively village communities in the Highlands, I was inwardly resigned to yet another run-through of an incomer's catalogue of delights. But as her experience unfolded I realised that a strong community could not always be assumed to be good news for anyone just turning up on its doorstep. For no reason she could identify, apart from her Englishness, this woman had been more or less shunned by her neighbours for the five years since she and her husband and family arrived. She has not been able to gain admittance to any informal child-care networks and during a period of immobilising illness when she says, 'I was desperate for a bit of help but didn't have the confidence to ask anyone,' she felt dreadfully isolated. She had come from an English city where she was used to giving and receiving support from an extended network of family and friends. Her husband's job had offered him and his family the chance to come to the Highlands and they had assumed that they would be able to take advantage of a strong rural community and all it had to offer in social terms. 'I've never felt lonely like I've felt lonely up here,' she confessed, gesturing to the panoramic view from her kitchen window. I heard the pain and resignation in her voice as she admitted to having no real idea why she should have been so comprehensively rejected. 'I find it really hard to accept it's just because I'm English. What have I done to anybody? I'm just a person...'

I had heard second-hand reports of such miseries among English incomers before but had chosen, probably for my own peace of mind, to ignore them. This woman's experience appeared to be indisputable proof that for some Highlanders, the English were, *a priori*, not welcome. To respect this interviewee's anonymity (which I do without a quibble) I can't say what her husband's job was. But I can say that he performed it outwith the community in which they had settled and, at first sight, it wasn't a life and death affair but one of those jobs which is only noticed when for some reason it's not being properly done. In other words, this family's contribution to Highland society was neither high profile or on the spot for the community into which they had so markedly failed to integrate.

I started the interviews because I was looking for answers to questions which were haunting me. However, it turned out that few interviewees were initially disposed to discuss the existence of the issues which were bothering me. Despite this reluctance, by the time each interview reached its final, most obviously political questions, even those Settlers most delighted with their views and lifestyles and all the other advantages they had secured by moving north did reveal at least a slight sense of their own vulnerability. Few, for example, were able to reject outright my analogy with Yugoslavia about what happens to different nationalities when the argument for consensus is fatally damaged by a decline in the power which has previously enforced such consensus. A small number argued, against me, that 'it couldn't happen here'. 'Yes, there's a theoretical possibility of nationalism erupting here if something went wrong with government functions,' admitted an English shop-owner surrounded, as he spoke, by thousands of pounds worth of stock. His words were enveloped in a hypothetical blandness as if he were talking about something which held no implications for him.

Others had done more serious thinking on the subject,

prompted by some less than idyllic experiences, in particular in the workplace. One couple had spent much of their working life in the Highlands, doing an impressive variety of jobs. They love Scotland too much to want to sound bitter, but they have had some difficult moments, which they described to me. 'It was like I was the embodiment of all that was wrong with English imperialism.' 'This is what it must be like being black.' 'As soon as I opened my mouth (and spoke in an unmistakably English accent) judgements were made.' One of them had had personal experience of the illogicalities of nationalist abuse. 'Am I English just because I've got an English accent? My Scottish grandparents were oppressed by England too!' Even the English proprietrix of an impressive and long-established croft/craft enterprise actually made these two statements at different moments in the same interview: 'I am constantly reminded I am English but I don't believe in changing your voice,' and 'Sometimes I do wish it [her English accent] wasn't so prominent.'

So, many of my interviewees did eventually reveal at least some of the negative aspects of what Highland life was like for them. However, there did emerge, by the time the interviews were finished, another set of exceptional interviewees who did go a long way to providing me with an answer to my own questions about how to belong and why the whole issue should even matter.

There were three interviewees in this group: a dry-stane dyker and general handyman, a nurse and a primary school teacher. Their stories were significantly different from the others in ways which I decided were definitely related. Most strikingly of all they weren't anything like as concerned about their anonymity as the other interviewees. Moreover, each of them had very little to say about politics, neither the personal ones of encountering racism, or wider issues like the fairness or relevance of the Union.

Peter Wright, jack-of-all-trades, lives with his family in the same steading I first moved to from England. The north of Scotland is his second long-term home since he left his native Somerset. He went to the Yorkshire Dales, disillusioned by the changes overtaking the south-west of England and degrading both the natural and social environment there. But the Dales did not prove immune to such changes and when tourism began to replace agriculture as the main economic reality there he was ready to move again. This time the Highlands were his destination and one which he continues to feel will be, for the most part, able to resist such changes.

He came originally to work for the new owners of a small, dilapidated estate in south-east Sutherland. They wanted expert assistance in restoring their property to economic viability and Peter had the right skills for the job. He had already experienced being an incomer in the highly traditional community of the Yorkshire Dales. Both there and in Sutherland the process of integration was made relatively straightforward by his ability, through his work as a dyker, fencer, shepherd and forester, to contribute to his new community in ways which it could easily understand and appreciate. Although in the Highlands the locals began by fixing on the ways his shepherding techniques differed from their own, they were soon impressed enough to respect and trust him. As proof of this, he quoted the verdict of one senior shepherd who told him, 'I've argued with every bugger in the north of Scotland but you and I have never fallen out.' And in the village below the steading, he reckoned he'd been inside nearly every house, *'fixing something.'* All this emerged as he responded to the first questions about how and why he had come to Scotland. These answers and digressions made questions about the success of his integration into Highland society seem quite redundant. He didn't seem particularly interested in discussing the state of the Union either. The political economy of his life in the

Highlands was congruent with what already existed in the Highlands before his arrival there. He did not make his living by producing commodities unfamiliar to the native inhabitants of his new home. 'It's the difference between being a feed rep and a candlemaker,' he mused, recalling his experiences as the Yorkshire Dales gradually lost what he called 'their vital spark' under the distorting pressures of tourism. Above all, he reckoned, 'I've made myself useful here.' It struck me, as I wove my way back next-door where I was staying the night (he'd been more than generous with his Famous Grouse) that the whole question of belonging to a place rather than simply happening to be there because of the nice view and the clean water could well boil down to something as simple as making oneself useful. What had s said about the need for rich foreigners to make a contribution?

I woke the next day already late for my interview with the Englishman who lived in the sombrely impressive Manse which had a breath-taking view of the Kyle of Sutherland where the Oykel and Carron rivers meet it and head for the North Sea. I knew Fred's reputation as something of a challenging thinker, so telling my hangover to pull itself together, I plugged in my tape-recorder at the Manse in full expectation of a positive account of the Church of Scotland and indeed Scottish radicalism as the powerful incentive which had brought Fred to train and work in Scotland. But though the view of the world from the Manse was not uninteresting, I felt rather disappointed to hear that the Minister had come to Scotland for a very pragmatic reason: the Church of Scotland, unlike the Church of England, allows divorced people to undertake training for the Ministry. He admitted to having felt somewhat daunted by the foreignness of his flock when he began his incumbency but he reckoned to have benefited from being thrown in at the deep end. 'There was an unusually high number of funerals the spring that I arrived and I think I was able to establish contact with a lot of people more quickly than I otherwise would.' Fred thought a lot of his parishioners and I knew they thought a lot of him, but I left the Manse not quite over the hangover and a bit depressed by the prospect of resuming the diet of interviews in which people merely listed all the reasons why the Highlands had proved such a convenient and agreeable place to settle. Of course it was good to hear that people were generally pleased with the choices they had made but sometimes that picture of total satisfaction did not convince me.

But my next port of call got rid of the depression and hangover. I was off to visit the District Nurse of some years work and residence in this Highland community. She was a chatty Geordie who had come regularly to the steading before and after my daughter was born. I would always enjoy a blether with Kathy and her official visits usually allowed time for a cup of tea and generally left me significantly wiser on key points of local information like who lived where and with whom and – well, you know the sort of thing.

I had Peter's phrase about the importance of making himself useful still very much in mind and I found I was talking to another incomer who as a triple duty nurse (Health Visitor, Midwife and District Nurse) had been far too busy making herself spectacularly useful to have any time to think about the political aspects of the Anglo-Scottish relationship. I couldn't imagine anyone who's just delivered a baby or given a painkilling injection or sorted an elderly patient's bedsores, being given a hard time about being English. Kathy's reasons for coming to live in the Highlands were voiced in terms of the practical contribution she intended to make. Visiting the area on holiday her first response to its beauty and character was to think, 'I'd like to work here.' She admitted to having been at a crossroads in her life at that point and was even considering going back to Bangladesh to work. She stressed she was not escaping to the Highlands: 'It was a job that I loved,' she said, but was just needing the challenge of a change of scene. And, when later in the interview, I asked her to tell me her feelings about Scottish history, she shook her head: 'It's now I'm interested in.'

Her new community had won her over immediately with its friendliness and relaxed atmosphere. She had also been most impressed by the up-to-date vibrancy of the local nursing profession, despite its distance from urban centres. 'It's only looking back that I see what a rat race life was down south, though I didn't come here to get away from it. Down there people don't take anything like such a personal interest in you as they do here.'

Talk of integration seemed superfluous here too. Kathy knew she was a valued and well-liked member of the community: she had even married a Highlander who is very much part of the local scene. 'Even if I hadn't married David, I would never think of going back. I definitely feel this is home.'

There was such a refreshing difference about Peter and Kathy's interviews that I found myself enthusiastic all over again about the whole interview project. Perhaps it could be interesting after all to look at how the English were making themselves at home in the Highlands. Moreover, the two interviews suggested the possibility of there being a workable solution to the whole problem of what the English might be able to do to cancel out the negative associations they inevitably brought with them when they crossed the Border: they could do something useful!

There is a sad but, I hope, not a wholly dismal footnote to be included here. Since Kathy gave me this interview she has finally lost her long and painful struggle against an illness which prematurely stopped her doing the job she did so well in the place she loved. She told me during the interview that the view of the Kyle of Sutherland from the northern side of Struie Hill always made her feel happy to be nearly home. I agreed and now will feel even fonder of that impressive, yet somehow human-scale view. More pertinent to the pivotal role her interview plays in this book is the fact (as I was told by my neighbour from the steading) that so many wanted to pay their respects at her funeral that they could not all get into the church. Knowing the area and the high esteem in which Kathy was held there, I'm sure the crowd will have contained English and Scots, locals and incomers. I'm equally sure that Kathy would not have even noticed.

I only found one more interviewee whose move to Scotland was underpinned by a real determination to contribute significantly to the country she had chosen as her own.

At first sight, Sophie was the epitome of the sort of incomer who chooses to use the Highlands as a stunning backdrop for her own spiritual agenda. She came to the Highlands on holiday after finishing University. She visited an established community whose goals were avowedly spiritual and whose personnel was usually one hundred percent non-Highlander. The group made its living from a variety of sources: they did some crofting, made and sold handcrafted items and filled the gaps with Social Security payments. In her post-University hiatus Sophie found the spiritual priorities of the community both inspiring and sustaining and she loved the Highland landscape and people. But rather than stay where she was and just hope for something to turn up, she returned to England for a year to work for a post-graduate primary school teaching qualification. She told me that she had never come up against anti-English feeling and it had certainly never been an issue at work. She was uninterested in the politics of the Union which she regarded with little emotional attachment, being the daughter of Irish immigrants to England. Here was another case which calls into question the actual Englishness of those who seem (that is, sound) English in the Highlands.

I have had no qualms about giving so much space to these

exceptions because most of the rest of the interviews contained much repetition and little imagination. Peter, Kathy and Sophie shared a singularity which the extracts you have read should have made obvious. However, there was one interview which showed in a coldly final way the complete vulnerability of all our arrogant delusions about the perfectibility of life. You know the sort of idea: all you have to do to get a brand new life is to change your clothes, or your job or house or lifestyle or why not do it all at once and change country. This interview demonstrates with horrid clarity that changing places may be the cue for more changes in your life than those you had in mind.

What were you most looking forward to in Scotland?

I came here to walk on the hills. There never seemed to be enough time on holiday to really make the most of the hills – you rushed up here in your car, rushed up as many as you could manage, always watching your schedule, crossing off as many as you could – and then you rushed home again. This hurry was slightly at odds with the silence and serenity you savoured on the tops. I hated being a tourist here – I thought I could belong simply by relocating on a permanent basis. Each return to England seemed like a journey in the wrong direction. As the land got flatter and busier, my spirit sank and the Highlands suddenly seemed like a fantastic dream. I wanted to make it real – a dream-come-true, I suppose. It feels like there's hardly anywhere in England which isn't all covered with asphalt, buildings, all the works of man. Your eyes crave emptiness and space, your soul wants peace and quiet; all that's what I was most looking for in Scotland.

Well, that seems to have covered the first four questions. Yes, well, like I said, I've had more than enough time to think about it all; enough time to try and make sense of my place in things, now my life and my options are all so totally changed. I felt quite confident that I had successfully anticipated all I would need to do to get used to living in Scotland. I never bargained for coping with the sort of changes I had to face because of becoming ill. Never even dreamt...

What do you miss about England now?

I guess what I miss doesn't really exist anymore – apart from in tiny pockets. England is so busy now, so full of people and much of the countryside is empty of life. The only country places which escape these changes are those which are, for whatever reason, impossible to make money out of: too wet to build on or plough up; too wet, too rocky, too high, too low or just too tricky to make someone a proper profit. These places give you glimpses of a vanished time which you know about because of books and what old country people say about the way things used to be. When I get nostalgic for England which doesn't happen very often, I guess it's generally for a place which is hardly there anymore...

Have your feelings about Scotland changed?

Well, my feelings about everything have changed. Getting ill like this takes the person you thought you were and turns it, plus all its assumptions and expectations upside down and inside out. It's fairly drastic: not so much like somebody's moved the goal posts, more like the total abolition of all ball-games.

So, thoughts about Scotland?

Well, the Scotland I came for has been denied me just as absolutely as if I'd been turned back at the Border and that made me feel desperately pissed off to begin with. You know, sometimes I almost wished I was back in England so I couldn't even see the hills any more. I couldn't come to terms with the idea that I could only look at the Highlands through a stuffy car's window, that I would never get to all those places which I had hoped to walk to. I bet you haven't interviewed anybody else who has cried their eyes out because of the *Dashing White Sergeant*? I was so looking forward to joining in the Scottish Country Dancing: we did it on rainy lunchtimes at Primary School. I had one shot at it here when I was still quite mobile; it was great, much wilder than Primary School, far more flirting – but I couldn't walk for a week afterwards. Never again! I'd sort of been relying on Scottish Country Dancing as a way to meet people and I'd felt the same about getting work on farms or in shops. Quite impossible now as you can see.

Over just a few dreadful months, Scotland went from being a heavenly playground to a hell where the landscape stopped being inspirational and turned to a tantalisingly unreachable reminder of why I had come, and why there was suddenly no reason to stay. So now it simply is the here and now which I must relish minute by minute or give up in despair... tricky, eh? But I have been forced to the discovery that the worthwhile project is not revelling in emptiness and space and thinking that's where to find God, but knowing that God must be found within wherever you are, whatever has happened to you. Bloody tricky, I say.

But, now I feel very lucky to be going through all this here. I visited the south of England last year – disastrous trip – it was springtime and the light was bright so you could tell it was springtime – but the horizons were all blurred; the air was kind of grimy, unclear... and the tap-water made my mouth taste sick. All us English Settlers have been spoiled by the purity of the environment up here: we can't bear to think of going back. And it wasn't only the environment that seemed suddenly alien. Everyone was screaming round convinced that what they were up to was the most important thing that had ever happened. Nobody but the nutters (and there were plenty of those) could take their eyes off the ball for a minute. Mind you, from what I hear, Inverness is going a bit that way.

Do you consider yourself English, Scottish, British or none of these?

Being ill like this forces you to realise how fragile and chancy our notions of our own identity are. I know that the facts of where you are born and how you were bred are accidents, the outer garments, if you like, of who we are. Being in this wheelchair makes me an outsider wherever I am; in comparison with which being English seems quite a trivial handicap.

Describe your feelings about Scottish history and culture.

I'm surprised at how little I know about Scottish history. It's bloody confusing: bloody and confusing! I'm still really turned on by the liveliness of Scottish culture. It seems much more important to people here, in the Highlands anyway, than the equivalent does anywhere I've lived in England. Here, more people are more enthusiastic about common ideas of what's worthwhile... even if the genuineness of some Scottish culture is a bit suspect. Apparently key bits like tartan and piping and Highland Games are all Victorian corruptions of the real thing. But I'm not quite sure how much that actually matters... what I like most about Scottish culture is the family feeling: a sort of shared familiarity which again is missing from England – certainly the south-east of it, anyway. It makes me very badly wish I could take part in Scottish culture somehow and get a taste of that familiarity. I am an outsider in so many ways now; being English is only one.

If you feel like going on there is one last question...

OK, I'm not going anywhere.

Describe your feelings about the Act of Union and if you would like to see any change would you favour Devolution or Independence.

When I was well I used to think that the best I could do was to promise to adopt Scottish citizenship as soon as I could. But the idea of that sort of statement seems ridiculous now that I am just a parcel of expensive requirements in a wheelchair. I'm just grateful to any country for letting me into its welfare system. I know I should be spouting on about rights rather than gratitude, but it feels more realistic just to be relieved. The Act of Union? Just another example of the world thinking things are the way they are because they've always been like that, and that's the best and fairest way for them to be. It makes me tired to think of it where I once would have been angry... I suppose I understand better now how people come to settle for what's unavoidable, even though they never would have chosen such an outcome.

CHAPTER 5

Jings! Or why I love the Guid Scots tongue

UP TO DATE NOW: a couple more flittings and suddenly I've been in the Highlands for ten years and most of the important people in my life are here though many of them, like me, were born elsewhere, either in Scotland, England or the whole wide world. Some of my closest moments with real (i.e. born and bred here) Highlanders are with the youngsters to whom I give English lessons to help them prepare for Scottish Examination Board exams. I still find myself thinking about the issues of blood and belonging which so preoccupied me when I first arrived; but, inevitably, the exigencies of the here and now take up most of my attention. Does that mean I'm integrated? Last year I was unwittingly provided with a possible answer to that question by a visitor from England. I don't get as many of these as I once did: the novelty of the destination has rather worn off with only very determined friendships surviving the distance from England.

Caroline's grandfather was a crofter and postman on the west coast of Sutherland. His daughter, Caroline's mother, was sent away to school in Edinburgh. She went on to train as a teacher there, only returning to the croft for holidays. Caroline was born in Leeds where her mother had married a lawyer and her childhood holidays were all spent on the croft. She grew to love the place, its people and its stunning views with a fierce and enduring passion.

I had put an advertisement in the local paper to try and buy a second-hand gas cooker and while Caroline was with me I answered several phone calls replying to it. The resulting conversations about gas bottles, cooker models and prices seemed ordinary to me but I noticed Caroline becoming increasingly agitated. Finally, her good manners cracked and I found out what was bothering her. 'I'm sorry,' she started, 'but it just sounds so bizarre to hear you coming out with all those ochs and ayes and where do you stays.'

She was smiling as she spoke yet I could sense her annoyance and I wanted to know exactly what she found so vexing.

'I know it's irrational,' she admitted, 'but it's just that I feel protective of Scotland and especially the Highlands; that's where those words and that way of saying them belong, not to you.'

I asked whether she had ever considered moving permanently to the Highlands as I had heard so much about the intense love she had for the place. Her answer was obviously the result of much hard thinking: 'I accept the Highlands was never my home, my physical home that is. It was my holiday home and life is not a holiday. It is my spiritual home and I still might...' She told me how she had heard all about the White Settlers and their weird and terrible ways from her Highland friends and relations whose baffled contempt alone had been enough to deter her from joining the ever-increasing ranks of English arrivals.

Might I have been less carelessly eager to come north if I had known more about the complications which awaited me? I had come though, and now I had learnt enough of the words to provoke in her the same indignant sense of incongruity that Ken and Rosemary, the Essex Highlanders, had done in me a decade earlier. I was reminded of that episode and wondered what actual difference those years had made to me beyond the mere accretion of a few words and phrases on to my own personal dialect. After all, wherever I've lived in England and Scotland, I, like most people, have picked up something of the local parlance. But though I've not acquired a Scottish accent, the Scottish usage and idioms I have adopted signify something different from previous linguistic borrowings. This difference depends on the fact that the way many Scots speak reflects some of the values which inform much of their country's society, and, in particular, that society's essential differences from England. There are few words used regularly in English public life which would not be easily understood by the hundreds of millions of members of the contemporary world-wide community of English-language speakers. Speakers of Scots from all arenas of public life seem glad to include in their discourse any number of Scots words which would probably baffle most English speakers including those in England. Moreover, as is most definitely not the case in England, the use of vernacular words by Scots speakers carries no implication of social inferiority. Neither Scots words nor a strong Scots accent has any automatically negative social connotations. Notably, in many instances I have observed that a strong Scots accent does not necessarily make for total incomprehensibility. The Doric accent of Aberdeenshire and the north-east, has more than once proved unintelligible to me and Glaswegian is sometimes delivered too quickly for outsiders to grasp. On the whole, however, Scottish people pronounce their accented speech most clearly, often sounding every syllable separately, even some syllables which (comparatively) dull English voices omit altogether. Naturally, I'm not going to account for these vocal phenomena by any notions of the Scots as somehow special but history and geography can go some way to explaining these national traits. The way Scots speak evolved largely at a distance from central authority, either in remote self-sufficient areas before the full development of the mass media or, later, in a land which viewed central authority (Westminster) as distant and essentially foreign. There was historically, therefore, little incentive for most Scots to smooth the rough edges of their language to make it comprehensible to those for whom it was unfamiliar. In any event, whether or not Scots derives its vividness and strength from its original development in an age when civilisation and all its comforts had not blunted our sensory perceptions, it contains lots of absolutely cracking words with vibrant descriptive qualities far surpassing much of what standard English has to offer.

I include here a list of them which is only intended as a taster for the uninitiated. A few general points must accompany it. First is the fact that the Scots language having first lost royal authority and patronage with the Regal Union of 1603, was then severely discouraged in Scottish schools in modern times. The language's country-wide survival is, therefore, all the more remarkable. Second, despite this troubled history, today the use of Scots is in all contexts socially and intellectually acceptable. Third, despite the closely-linked historical relationship generally agreed to exist between the English and Scots languages, there are many Scots words which lack a satisfactory equivalent in English. This simple fact underpins the critical idea, the lesson which the English must learn: Scotland and England are different and separate places despite their proximity and the many similarities they undoubtedly share.

The following list is a short selection of quintessentially Scots words for which no one-word English alternative can be satisfactorily rendered:

kenspeckle	familiar or easily spotted
clamjamfrie	miscellany of people or things
dreich	bleak, miserable, boring
to *swither*	to be in a state of indecision and/or confusion
clashmaclavers	gossip

The marvellous sound of these words, their multiple meanings and sophisticated nuances make the search for a worthy English equivalent quite hopeless. If the weather is bleak or miserable, it's a great consolation to be able to pronounce it dreich. For a sample of the vivid rhythm of contemporary Scots prose, readers, if they can thole (put up with/endure) the gory details of contemporary urban heroin addiction should look at Irvine Welsh's *Trainspotting*. But for a taste of Scots where unfamiliar words don't come in indigestible and confusing chunks but, rather, illuminate and ornament a powerful humanist narrative, try Lewis Grassic Gibbon's 1932 trilogy, A *Scots Quair*. If you fall in love with Grassic Gibbon's descriptions of the Howe of the Mearns in *Sunset Song*, the first volume of the trilogy, discovering that he wrote the entire three volumes while living in Welwyn Garden City may surprise you. He had spent years in the British Army during which time he wrote fantastical stories in stilted English which gained little recognition at the time and none since. A *Scots Quair* is written in a uniquely rewarding mixture of Scots and English, which remains accessible to a general readership while retaining the vivid excitement of the *speak* of Aberdeenshire.

> Now Peesie's Knapp's biggings were not more than twenty years old, but gey ill-favoured for all that, for though the house faced on the road - and that was fair handy if it didn't scunner you that you couldn't so much as change your sark without some ill-fashioned brute gowking in at you – right between the byre and the stable and the barn on one side and the house on the other was the cattle-court and right in the middle of that the midden, high and yellow with dung and straw and sharn, and Mistress Strachan could never forgive Peesie's Knapp because of that awful smell it had.

biggings	buildings
gey ill-favoured	very unattractive to look at
scunner	disgust
sark	shirt
gowking	staring foolishly
sharn	fresh dung

For a different sample of the Scots tongue, I would choose

another text: *The New Testament* translated into Scots by William Laughton Lorimer. As a result of the complexities of Scottish Reformation politics and, in particular, John Knox's own Anglophile preferences, Scotland's Reformation did not produce a widely adopted vernacular version of any part of *The Bible*. A distinguished classical translator, Lorimer remedied this omission by devoting a lifetime to translating the original Greek of The New Testament into Scots. His work stands as a compelling monument to the power of that language. This is Lorimer's rendering of *Matthew, Chapter 7, v. 13-19*:

> Gae ye in at the nairrow yett. Side an wide is the gate at leads tae sculder, an monie feck traivels it: but nairrow is the yett, an nae braider is the gate, at leads til life; an no monie finnds it.

> Be-waur o fauss prophets at come tae ye in sheep's cleadin, but aneth is ravenish woufs. Ye will ken them bi their deeds. Div fowk gether grapes aff briar-busses, or fegs aff thrissles? Na, fy: ilka guid tree beirs guid frute, an ilka rotten tree beirs ill frute. A guid tree canna beir ill frute, nor a rotten tree guid frute. Ilka tree at beirsna guid frute is cuttit doun an cuissen intil the fire. Sae ye will ken thir men bi their frute.

RLC Lorimer, son of William, edited his father's mighty work of translation after his death. In his introduction he recalls his father's rendering of Matthew's account of The Temptation in which he gave The Devil English words to speak. William Lorimer did not, however, consider publishing this version.

My final helping of the glory that is the Scots language is taken from the work of the man who is that language's most famous and most universally loved exemplar, Robert Burns. In the late 1780s when fashionable Edinburgh was falling over itself to expunge all traces of Scots from its speech, English elocution teachers flocked north in droves to assist with the process. Simultaneously, however, the best-selling star of the Scottish literary scene was the Ploughman Poet, Robert Burns. His first and greatest collection of poems, published in Kilmarnock in 1786, was entitled *Poems, chiefly in the Scots Dialect*. Its contents included original poems by Burns as well as his reworkings of traditional Scottish songs. This apparently paradoxical attitude of the Scottish intellectual élite to the Scots language also existed in the work of Burns himself. Some of his poems use little or no Scots at all while many are a remarkable blend of sophisticated English and vigorous Scots. His father had joined with other parents to engage a tutor who gave the young Burns a solid grounding in all that the contemporary English literary world revered. This involved becoming familiar with the classics and learning to use language to express many fine nuances of emotion. Burns' creative genius was able to take what it wanted from the best on both sides of the linguistic border. Yet it is the Scots language used by Burns which illuminates his most memorable qualities as a poet. These include his abundant sympathies for and support of the real virtue innate in ordinary men and women as well as the mordant accuracy of his satire. This is consistently directed against conditions and institutions which stifle or pervert human potential. The poem included here as an example of the glorious power of Burns' Scots could have been any one of the scores of Burns' poetic masterpieces. *For a' that and a' that* seems, however, particularly to contain attitudes which the Scots voice has traditionally expressed: a detestation of the way freedom falls prey to the strangleholds of inequality and vested interests as well as a Scots contempt for people who hold unmerited power or position. Notice how the Scots words in the poem mark its emotional high points. Burns' ironic use of *birkie*, (a lively, spry fellow) emphasises the scorn he feels for such figures' pretensions to dignity and the iniquitous system they depend on and represent.

The *birkie's* ludicrous actions stress this scorn further. To eliminate any remaining doubt about the way Burns despises this figure and everything he stands for, the poet describes him with a Scots word, *coof*, meaning fool, clown or lout. Note the Scots word's powerful onomatopoeia: a single syllable of cutting contempt. The title and recurring verbal *leitmotiv* demonstrates the strength Scots derives from its informality. At once accessible and slightly disrespectful, the repetition of *a'* meaning 'all' leaves us in no doubt that the poem has not been inspired by self-serving ambition or personal antagonism but is speaking for the common good, for *a'*.

> *For a' that and a' that*
> *Is there, for honest Poverty*
> *That hings his head, and a' that;*
> *The coward-slave, we pass him by,*
> *We dare be poor for a' that!*
> *For a' that, and a' that,*
> *Our toils obscure, and a' that,*
> *The rank is but the guinea's stamp,*
> *The Man's the gowd for a' that.*
>
> *What though on hamely fare we dine,*
> *Wear hoddin grey, and a' that.*
> *Gie fools their silks, and knaves their wine,*
> *A Man's a Man for a' that.*
> *For a' that, and a' that,*
> *Their tinsel show, and a' that;*
> *The honest man, though e'er sae poor,*
> *Is king o' men for a' that.*

Ye see yon birkie ca'd, a lord,
Wha struts, and stares, and a' that,
Though hundreds worship at his word,
He's but a coof for a' that,
For a' that, and a' that,
His ribband, star and a' that
The man of independant mind,
He looks and laughs at a' that.

A prince can mak a belted knight,
A marquis, duke, and a' that;
But an honest man's aboon his might,
Gude faith he mauna fa' that!
For a' that, and a' that,
Their dignities, and a' that;
The pith o' sense and pride of o' worth,
Are higher rank than a' that.

Then let us pray that come it may,
As come it will for a' that,
That Sense and Worth, o'er a' the earth
Shall bear the gree, and a' that.
For a' that, and a' that
It's comin' yet for a' that,
That Man to Man the warld o'er
Shall brothers be for a' that.'

One of the great assets Scots has as a literary language must be its vividly colloquial nature. My experience of the spoken Scottish voice has been colloquial rather than literary, but it is in that everyday context that one of Scots' special jewels is to be found. The one word, the proud possession of which distinguishes Scots from English is *och*. Translating it to the pallidly impotent English oh demonstrates its impressive quality as a multi-purpose wordless emphasis for a vast range of emotional states: sorrow, anger, despair, affirmation, sympathy, exultation, frustration, contempt, reassurance, self-reproach... *Och* can carry an irresistible eloquence deriving from the speaker's decision to use feeling rather than words to underline what he or she is wanting to express. If an element of horror or disgust is required then *och* can become *ach* and the same wordless triumph occurs. The satisfying expressiveness of both *och* and *ach* is highly contagious. Ken and Rosemary couldn't stop interjecting it in 1987 and now I'm exactly the same, using it and the regular cast of Scots words and phrases which made Caroline wince when she heard them. If I think about my use of them for too long I wince too, but it would take a superhuman effort to eradicate them from my speech. I've caught *och* and *aye* and a host of other words and phrases. A particular favourite of mine is, 'On you go!' This is a delightfully positive equivalent of the pedestrian English 'Get on!' or 'Get on with you!' I didn't practise any of these words in private or attempt to manufacture a Scots accent with which to pronounce them: they just appeared as I talked to a lot of folk (there's another one of my Scots favourites: so much warmer than the formal English people) who use them all the time. If language is one aspect of a country's spirit then I think what has happened to the way I speak over the last ten years may well be some sort of integration after all.

But what about Gaelic? At the end of the eleventh century, Gaelic was spoken by most people in Scotland. Even now each hill, corrie, burn and brae in the Highlands has a Gaelic name.

Here are some examples:

Meall nan Caorach	Hill of the sheep
Aultbea (allt beithe)	The birch stream
Balachulish (bail' a'chaolais)	Town at the narrows
Loch an Airigh Fraoich	Loch of the heather sheiling (summer pasture)
Coille an Rois	The wood on the promontory or the seed wood

These are not the poetic appellations which the Victorian enthusiasts of Gaelic folklore might have expected but, rather, factually descriptive geographical references, vital for a culture whose survival depended on successful navigation and use of their natural environment. At the end of the twentieth century, White and Grey Settlers are walking their well-fed dogs, playing golf and building bungalows in a Highland landscape which was once intimately known and catalogued by the Gaelic speakers to whom the territory belonged before the nascent British Empire neutralised, traversed and renamed it with garrisons, bridges and roads. There are holiday complexes and plans for a hi-tec intensive pig farm on Drumossie Moor, the final resting place of Jacobite hopes and of many of the Gaels who were sacrificed to them. Back on the island of Raasay for the last time: I hear there's a New Age Develop-your-Spiritual-Potential Centre there now. Can its clients achieve sufficient awareness to catch the sound of thatches crackling and cattle bellowing with fright as English Marines exact Cumberland's revenge on the tiny green island? Does the posing of such a question constitute unnecessary wallowing in the historical mire? Unnecessary it may be to any New Age self-improvement project but not to the meaningful integration into contemporary Highland life of English incomers. Such outsiders, hopeful of belonging, may be misled by the apparent comprehensibility and relative familiarity of much that makes up life in the Highlands: they may be lulled into believing that the north of Scotland is unconditionally available to them as a glorious setting for whatever their aspirations are. If England did learn more about Scotland past, present and future than it knows at the moment, then future English arrivals might be able to dispense with their impedimenta of misconceptions before setting out. Moreover, the chances of equitable relations being established between England and Scotland might well be more likely, given the benefit of more educated popular demand for and scrutiny of such relations.

CHAPTER 6

The Last Weekend

WHEN I FIRST SETTLED in the Highlands, I fantasised about getting a t-shirt printed with 'The Clearances were not my fault' on the front and 'Lifelong anti-Tory voter' on the back. As Conservative cackhandedness and insensitivity lost the party credibility throughout Scotland, more than ever I felt bound to explain that I, at least, wanted none of its reactionary, divisive inadequacies. But to whom should I explain all this and how? Take out an ad in *The Ross-shire Journal*? Learn the Highland pipes? Get a tattoo, 'I ♡ the Assynt Crofters'? Join the Scottish National Party?

Well, I wrote this book instead. The questionnaire which was originally conceived as the book's centrepiece was, I now recognise, only made up of all the questions I would like to answer publicly in order to show that I took nothing for granted in my new home.

However, the historical survey I compiled of a thousand years of Scotland's relations with England which the project had seemed to demand made it glaringly obvious that wearing a t-shirt or making any superficial gesture wasn't enough to mitigate a millennium or so of English bully-boy behaviour. So I carried on with the book, attempting to keep one eye on the saga of the English behaving badly toward Scotland. The way the episodes were going only served to increase my motivation to continue. But now as the last weekend of writing is upon me, history is about to intervene to upstage my two years of intermittent scribbling about how things might be different. Yes, it's Referendum time!

New Labour's Referendum on the setting up of a Scottish Parliament should put an end to the century of procrastination and prevarication with which the Westminster Parliament has treated

Friday 29th August 1997

I've got to sort out the weekend. I want to finish writing before a new week begins, even the bibliography and 'Thanks to' bit. I've got to fit in a couple of English lessons and play guitar for Scotland Forward who are taking an open-topped bus to Inverness to drum up (strum up) plenty of Yes/Yes's. I ring up the local organiser to check when and where the bus is setting off, and to ask, on behalf of a journalist I know who's coming up from London to do an eve-of-Referendum piece on the English in Scotland, if there are any English people in her organisation to whom he can talk. Her answer seems to fulfil all my hopes that the fairness promised by a Scottish Parliament will begin to erode Scottish resentment of the English.

At first she pauses, then admits, 'I'm not sure who is English. It's never occurred to me to distinguish... It's just not an issue we're interested in.' As I hear those words, pronounced in a clear Scots accent, I realise I don't have to go on being interested in it either. Now, as the woman from Scotland Forward agrees, it's not a question of asking who is Scots or English but of asking who believes in Scotland's future as a country free from domination by a Westminster agenda. No doubt plenty of native Scots will vote No/No but I am as qualified as they are to be part of the decision-making which could be the start of a new era in Scottish self-determination. Moreover, I get to play my guitar on the top of the bus and make visible to all which side I am on.

I heard an English woman from Dumfries (further from the Highlands than some of England) talking on Radio Scotland about the Referendum. She was being apologetic which I didn't like the sound of at all. 'I'm not going to vote; I don't feel I'm in a position to make this decision as it's not my home.' A part of me acknowledged the basic truth of this but then I remembered Peter

Wright and Kathy. If we live here then we must be involved enough to vote at meetings. That's the trouble with English politeness: its excessiveness can lose the point of politeness all together and politeness which misses the point isn't politeness at all. All I want is for the day to come when there is nothing to be polite about.

But this new world of freedom and harmony can't happen overnight. On my way home from the bus I hear about an English-born Black Isle schoolboy who got into a scrap after he was taunted for being English and is now too scared to leave his house. And in the *Herald* there is a front page report about a new group called *English Rights Scotland* formed by English-born people resident in Scotland who claim to be suffering from a 'rising tide of hostility'. Indeed the same article announces a marked rise in English complaints of racial harassment and prejudice. These now constitute 10% of the complaints received by the Edinburgh-based Commission for Racial Equality, a figure which has risen from 2% over the last three years. It will be no surprise if a thousand years of trouble can't be forgotten overnight. However, the Devolution Referendum must usher in the start of a different time when Scots no longer have to labour under what they perceive as institutionalised iniquities. Of course, how it all works out in practice remains to be seen.

Sunday 31st August

Yesterday's euphoric certainties evaporate instantly with the shocking news of Princess Diana's death. Her status as icon swells by the minute and I'm surprised, as no great fan of Royalty, to find myself brimming over with tears even while despising the blanket media coverage of the event and reactions to it as excessive. But straight away I'm wondering: What about the Referendum? How will this news, which seems more important with every minute, affect the result. All Referendum campaigning is called off until the Monday before the poll which leaves only a hundred hours. How will this intense mourning of the Princess affect the outcome? My heart sinks as I imagine this event and the extraordinary reaction it has provoked skewing the whole vote. A hundred years of waiting and yet another chance lost? But how do the Scots actually feel about Princess Diana's death? It is a shock to discover that I don't really have a clue about how much Scots will be touched by what has happened in Paris. Scotland has certainly had some powerful moments with the British Royal family over the years. Butcher Cumberland, for starters, took a special interest in demonstrating exactly how the Union was going to work out in practice. But after this savage Hanoverian episode, the Royals kept falling in love with Scotland. Cumberland's nephew, George IV, came to Edinburgh in 1822, arriving at Leith by Royal yacht. Sir Walter Scott, British patriot *par exellence* organised and presided over the visitation which featured parades, receptions and much pageantry. He had persuaded the King to adopt Highland dress, long since free of Cumberland's vicious prohibition. The state of His Majesty's legs obliged him to favour tights under what was apparently a shorter than usual kilt. The King stayed a fortnight in the city whose people received him favourably.

Queen Victoria was the next British monarch to dally seriously with Scotland. Her connection with Balmoral seems to have played a very important part in her life especially after she became a widow at the age of forty-two. Lady Elizabeth Bowes-Lyons came from an anciently aristocratic Scots family to strengthen and adorn the Royal family as Queen through dark and difficult days and her grandson, Charles, seems very much at home on Deeside in his kilt. He even went crofting on Berneray in the Outer

Hebrides in happier times. So what do all these different Royal connections tell me about Scottish attitudes to the British Royal family at this critical moment? Does a nation made up of 'Jock Tamson's bairns', as the Scots describe their own particular slice of common humanity, regard a family defined by its unique hereditary possessions of privilege and wealth? Will the mourning for Diana require everyone to drape themselves in the Union flag? Or will it have the opposite effect as people remember how the Wales's fairytale marriage ended so shabbily? The surprisingly shocking event in Paris has caught me out badly, not only in my tendency to mist over when I think of dead Diana and her motherless children, but, less emotionally, in my absolute ignorance of what difference all this will make to the Referendum. As Sunday ticks slowly by I try tuning into Radio Scotland but all BBC radio seems to be mourning Diana. All sorts of folk are being wheeled on to lament her passing; the layers of sentimentality and hypocrisy begin to stick in my throat. In desperation I flick back to Radio Scotland, just in case... and it's as if a window has been flung open and sunlight and a cool mountain breeze have poured in, instantly dispersing what has gone before. It's a programme on the songs of Robert Burns: that arch-opponent of sentimentalism who celebrated and dignified the range of human emotional experience and who despised any person or idea that attempted to restrict or deny that experience. The songs, with simple piano accompaniment, make a perfect antidote for the overblown emotional rhetoric which has taken over the air-waves. Yet again I am terrifically grateful for the fresh air of Scotland.

11th September

It's nearly midnight and I don't feel hopeful enough of the outcome to stay awake for the Referendum results on the radio. When I went to register my Yes/Yes, the polling station was deserted and the man in charge laughed out loud when I asked if he'd been busy. The media's summary of the day also suggested a low turn-out and a general reluctance to support tax-raising powers for the new Assembly. The euphoria of the campaign bus had all but evaporated.

How would we ever live with ourselves and each other if we didn't get it right this time?

Bibliography

Imagined Communities: Reflections on the Origin and Spread of Nationalism, Benedict Anderson, Verso Editions, 1991

Blood and Belonging: Journeys into the New Nationalism, Michael Ignatieff, BBC Books, 1993

A New History of Scotland, G.S Pryde and W. Croft Dickinson, 2 Vols., Nelson, 1961

A Description of the Western Islands of Scotland, Martin Martin, 1703, reprinted by Birlinn, 1994

A Journey to the Western Islands of Scotland, Samuel Johnson, 1775, reprinted Penguin, 1984

Britons: Forging the Nation, 1707-1837, Linda Colley, Yale University Press, 1992

Scotland and the Union, David Daiches, John Murray, 1976

Glencoe, John Prebble, Penguin, 1968

Culloden, John Prebble, Secker and Warburg, 1961

The Highland Clearances, John Prebble, Secker and Warburg, 1963

No Great Mischief if you Fall, John MacLeod, Mainstream, 1993

Highland Songs of the Forty-Five, ed. John Lorne Campbell, Gaelic Texts Society, 1984

Deer Forests, Landlords and Crofters in the Western Highlands, Willie Orr, John Donald, 1982

The Crofters' War, I.M.M. MacPhail, Acair, 1989

The Battle for Scotland, Andrew Marr, Penguin, 1992

Spade among the Rushes, Margaret Leigh, Birlinn, 1996

Who Owns Scotland, Andy Wightman, Canongate, 1996

The Continuum Concept, Jean Liedloff, Penguin, 1989

The Collins Encyclopaedia of Scotland, John and Julia Keay, Collins, 1994

Selected Poetry of Robert Burns, ed. Angus Calder and William Donnelly, Penguin, 1961

The Golden Treasury of Scottish Poetry, ed. Hugh MacDiarmid, Macmillan, 1948

Selected Poetry of Hugh MacDiarmid, ed. Alan Riach and Michael Grieve, Carcanet, 1992

The Company I've Kept, Hugh MacDiarmid, Hutchinson, 1966

A Highland Life, Neil Gunn, J.B. Pick and R. Hart, Polygon, 1981

A Scots Quair, Lewis Grassic Gibbon, Canongate, 1995

The New Testament in Scots, translated by William Laughton Lorimer, Penguin, 1985

Trainspotting, Irvine Welsh, Minerva, 1993

Why Scots Should Rule Scotland, Alasdair Gray, Canongate, 1992

Scots: The Mither Tongue, Billy Kay, Mainstream, 1986

The Story of English, R. McCrum, W. Cran and R MacNeil, Faber and Faber/BBC Books, revised and published 1992

A Scots School Dictionary, Chambers, 1996

Acknowledgements

For permission to reprint verse and prose extracts the publishers gratefully acknowledge the following:

Doubleday, a division of Transworld Publishers Ltd for the extract from *Behind the Scenes at the Museum* © Kate Atkinson 1995;

Canongate Books Ltd for *Who Owns Scotland* by Andy Wightman, *Sunset Song* by Lewis Grassic Gibbon and *The New Testament in Scots* translated by William Laughton Lorimer;

Birlinn Ltd for *Spade among the Rushes* by Margaret Leigh;

John Donald for *The Highland Bagpipe and its Music* by Roderick Cannon;

Random House for *The Company I've Kept* by Hugh MacDiarmid;

Carcanet Press for *A Drunk Man Looks at the Thistle* by Hugh MacDiarmid;

Malcolm Slessor and David Cooper Crane for excerpts from their report for Edinburgh University's Centre for Human Ecology;

General Register Office (Scotland) for permission to use their figures as a basis for the table on English-born residents in the Highlands.

ACKNOWLEDGEMENTS

The author is particularly grateful to Dr Richard Cox of the
Gaelic Texts Society for his help and advice and the permission
given by the Society for the publishers to reprint *Song of the Exiles*
by John MacCodrom translated by Rev. William Mathieson; also
Song of the Highland Clans by Alexander MacDonald and *Song
to the Breeches* by Duncan Ban MacIntyre, both translated by
John Lorne Campbell. These last two translations have been
reproduced with permission from John Lorne Campbell's literary
executrix, Margaret Fay Shaw.

Some other books published by **LUATH** PRESS

LUATH GRAPHICS

Old Scotland New Scotland

Jeff Fallow

ISBN 0 946487 40 5 PBK £6.99

'Together we can build a new Scotland based on Labour's values.' DONALD DEWAR, Party Political Broadcast

'Despite the efforts of decent Mr Dewar, the voters may yet conclude they are looking at the same old hacks in brand new suits.' IAN BELL, *The Independent*

'At times like this you suddenly realise how dangerous the neglect of Scottish history in our schools and universities may turn out to be.' MICHAEL FRY, *The Herald*

'...one of the things I hope will go is our chip on the shoulder about the English... The SNP has a huge responsibility to articulate Scottish independence in a way that is pro-Scottish and not anti-English.' ALEX SALMOND, *The Scotsman*

Scottish politics have never been more exciting. In *old Scotland new Scotland* Jeff Fallow takes us on a graphic voyage through Scotland's turbulent history, from earliest times through to the present day and beyond. This fast-track guide is the quick way to learn what your history teacher didn't tell you, essential reading for all who seek an understanding of Scotland and its history.

Eschewing the romanticisation of his country's past, Fallow offers a new perspective on an old nation. 'Too many people associate Scottish history with tartan trivia or outworn romantic myth. This book aims to blast that stubborn idea.' JEFF FALLOW

BIOGRAPHY

Tobermory Teuchter: A first-hand account of life on Mull in the early years of the 20th century

Peter Macnab

ISBN 0 946487 41 3 PBK £7.99

Peter Macnab was reared on Mull, as was his father, and his grandfather before him. In this book he provides a revealing account of life on Mull during the first quarter of the 20th century, focusing especially on the years of World War I. This enthralling social history of the island is set against Peter Macnab's early years as son of the governor of the Mull Poorhouse, one of the last in the Hebrides, and is illustrated throughout by photo-graphs from his exceptional collec-tion. Peter Macnab's 'fisherman's yarns' and other personal reminis-cences are told delightfully by a born storyteller. This latest work from the author of a range of books about the island, including the standard study of Mull and Iona, reveals his unparalleled knowledge of and deep feeling for Mull and its people. After his long career with the Clydesdale Bank, first in Tobermory and later on the mainland, Peter, now 94, remains a teuchter at heart, proud of his island heritage.

'Peter Macnab is a man of words who doesnit mince his words - not where his beloved Mull is concerned. 'I will never forget some of the inmates of the poorhouse,' says Peter. 'Some of them were actually victims of the later Clearances. It was history at first hand, and there was no romance about it'. But Peter Macnab sees little creative point in crying over ancient injustices. For him the task is to help Mull in this century and beyond.'
SCOTS MAGAZINE, May 1998

Bare Feet and Tackety Boots

Archie Cameron
ISBN 0 946487 17 0 PBK £7.95

The island of Rum before the First World War was the playground of its rich absentee landowner. A survivor of life a century gone tells his story. Factors and schoolmasters, midges and poaching, deer, ducks and MacBrayne's steamers: here social history and personal anecdote create a record of a way of life gone not long ago but already almost forgotten. This is the story the gentry couldn't tell.

'This book is an important piece of social history, for it gives an insight into how the other half lived in an era the likes of which will never be seen again'
FORTHRIGHT MAGAZINE

'The authentic breath of the pawky, country-wise estate employee.'
THE OBSERVER

'Well observed and detailed account of island life in the early years of this century'
THE SCOTS MAGAZINE

'A very good read with the capacity to make the reader chuckle. A very talented writer.'
STORNOWAY GAZETTE

On the Trail of Robert Service

GW Lockhart
ISBN 0 946487 24 3 PBK £7.99

Robert Service is famed world-wide for his eye-witness verse-pictures of the Klondike goldrush. As a war poet, his work outsold Owen and Sassoon, and he went on to become the world's first million selling poet. In search of adventure and new experiences, he emigrated from Scotland to Canada in 1890 where he was caught up in the aftermath of the raging gold fever. His vivid dramatic verse bring to life the wild, larger than life characters of the gold rush Yukon, their bar-room brawls, their lust for gold, their trigger-happy gambles with life and love. 'The Shooting of Dan McGrew' is perhaps his most famous poem:

A bunch of the boys were whooping it up in the Malamute saloon;
The kid that handles the music box was hitting a ragtime tune;

Back of the bar in a solo game, sat
Dangerous Dan McGrew,
And watching his luck was his light
o'love, the lady that's known as Lou.

His storytelling powers have brought
Robert Service enduring fame,
particularly in North America and
Scotland where he is something of a
cult figure.

Starting in Scotland, *On the Trail of
Robert Service* follows Service as he
wanders through British Columbia,
Oregon, California, Mexico, Cuba,
Tahiti, Russia, Turkey and the
Balkans, finally 'settling' in France.

This revised edition includes an
expanded selection of illustrations of
scenes from the Klondike as well as
several photographs from the family
of Robert Service on his travels
around the world.

Wallace Lockhart, an expert on
Scottish traditional folk music and
dance, is the author of *Highland Balls
& Village Halls* and *Fiddles & Folk*. His
relish for a well-told tale in popular
vernacular led him to fall in love with
the verse of Robert Service and write
his biography.

'*A fitting tribute to a remarkable man -
a bank clerk who wanted to become a
cowboy. It is hard to imagine a bank
clerk writing such lines as:
A bunch of boys were whooping it up...
The income from his writing actually
exceeded his bank salary by a factor of
five and he resigned to pursue a full time
writing career.*' Charles Munn,
THE SCOTTISH BANKER

'*Robert Service claimed he wrote for
those who wouldnit be seen dead reading
poetry. His was an almost unbelievably
mobile life... Lockhart hangs on*

*breathlessly, enthusiastically unearthing
clues to the poet's life.*' Ruth Thomas,
SCOTTISH BOOK COLLECTOR

'*This enthralling biography will delight
Service lovers in both the Old World and
the New.*' Marilyn Wright,
SCOTS INDEPENDENT

Come Dungeons Dark

John Taylor Caldwell
ISBN 0 946487 19 7 PBK £6.95

 Glasgow anarchist
Guy Aldred died
with 10p in his pock-
et in 1963 claiming
there was better
company in Barlin-
nie Prison than in
the Corridors of
Power. 'The Red Scourge' is remembered here by one who worked with
him and spent 27 years as part of his
turbulent household, sparring with
Lenin, Sylvia Pankhurst and others as
he struggled for freedom for his
beloved fellow-man.

'*The welcome and long-awaited
biography of... one of this country's
most prolific radical propagandists...
Crank or visionary?... whatever the
verdict, the Glasgow anarchist has
finally been given a fitting memorial.*'
THE SCOTSMAN

LUATH GUIDES TO SCOTLAND

These guides are not your traditional where-to-stay and what-to-eat books. They are companions in the rucksack or car seat, providing the discerning traveller with a blend of fiery opinion and moving description. Here you will find

'that curious pastiche of myths and legend and history that the Scots use to describe their heritage… what battle happened in which glen between which clans; where the Picts sacrificed bulls as recently as the 17th century… A lively counterpoint to the more standard, detached guidebook… Intriguing.'
THE WASHINGTON POST

These are perfect guides for the discerning visitor or resident to keep close by for reading again and again, written by authors who invite you to share their intimate knowledge and love of the areas covered.

Highways and Byways in Mull and Iona

Peter Macnab
ISBN 0 946487 16 2 PBK £4.25

'The Isle of Mull is of Isles the fairest,
Of ocean's gems 'tis the first and rarest.'
So a local poet described it a hundred years ago, and this recently revised guide to Mull and sacred Iona, the most accessible islands of the Inner Hebrides, takes the reader on a delightful tour of these rare ocean

gems, travelling with a native whose unparalleled knowledge and deep feeling for the area unlock the byways of the islands in all their natural beauty.

South West Scotland

Tom Atkinson
ISBN 0 946487 04 9 PBK £4.95

This descriptive guide to the magical country of Robert Burns covers Kyle, Carrick, Galloway, Dumfries-shire, Kirkcudbrightshire and Wigtownshire. Hills, unknown moors and unspoiled beaches grace a land steeped in history and legend and portrayed with affection and deep delight.

An essential book for the visitor who yearns to feel at home in this land of peace and grandeur.

The Lonely Lands

Tom Atkinson
ISBN 0 946487 10 3 PBK £4.95

A guide to Inveraray, Glencoe, Loch Awe, Loch Lomond, Cowal, the Kyles of Bute and all of central Argyll written with insight, sympathy and loving detail. Once Atkinson has taken you there, these lands can never feel lonely. 'I have sought to make the complex simple, the beautiful accessible and the strange familiar,' he writes, and indeed he brings to the land a knowledge and affection only accessible to someone with intimate knowledge of the area.

A must for travellers and natives who want to delve beneath the surface.

'Highly personal and somewhat quirky... steeped in the lore of Scotland.'
THE WASHINGTON POST

this guide to the Far West and Far North of Scotland. An unspoiled land of mountains, lochs and silver sands is brought to the walker's toe-tips (and to the reader's fingertips) in this stark, serene and evocative account of town, country and legend.

For any visitor to this Highland wonderland, Queen Victoria's favourite place on earth.

The Empty Lands

Tom Atkinson
ISBN 0 946487 13 8 PBK £4.95

The Highlands of Scotland from Ullapool to Bettyhill and Bonar Bridge to John O'Groats are landscapes of myth and legend, 'empty of people, but of nothing else that brings delight to any tired soul,' writes Atkinson. This highly personal guide describes Highland history and landscape with love, compassion and above all sheer magic.

Essential reading for anyone who has dreamed of the Highlands.

Roads to the Isles

Tom Atkinson
ISBN 0 946487 01 4 PBK £4.95
Ardnamurchan, Morvern, Morar, Moi-dart and the west coast to Ulla-pool are included in

FICTION

The Bannockburn Years

William Scott
ISBN 0 946487 34 0 PBK £7.95

A present day Edinburgh solicitor stumbles across reference to a document of value to the Nation State of Scotland. He tracks down the document on the Isle of Bute, a document which probes the real 'quaestiones' about nationhood and national identity. The document ends up being published, but is it authentic and does it matter? Almost 700 years on, these 'quaestiones' are still worth asking.

Written with pace and passion, William Scott has devised an intriguing vehicle to open up new ways of looking at the future of Scotland and its people. He presents an alternative inter-pretation of how the Battle of Bannockburn was fought, and through the Bannatyne manuscript he draws the reader into the minds of those involved.

Winner of the 1997 Constable Trophy, the premier award in Scotland for an unpublished novel, this book offers new insights to both the academic and the general reader which are sure to provoke further discussion and debate.

'A brilliant storyteller. I shall expect to see your name writ large hereafter.'
NIGEL TRANTER, October 1997.

'... a compulsive read.' PH Scott, THE SCOTSMAN

The Great Melnikov

Hugh MacLachlan
ISBN 0 946487 42 1 PBK £7.95

A well crafted, gripping novel, written in a style reminiscent of John  Buchan and set in London and the Scottish Highlands during the First World War, *The Great Melnikov* is a dark tale of double-cross and deception. We first meet Melnikov, one-time star of the German circus, languishing as a down-and-out in Trafalgar Square. He soon finds himself drawn into a tortuous web of intrigue. He is a complex man whose personal struggle with alcoholism is an inner drama which parallels the tense twists and turns as a spy mystery unfolds. Melnikov's options are narrowing. The circle of threat is closing. Will Melnikov outwit the sinister enemy spy network? Can he summon the will and the wit to survive?

Hugh MacLachlan, in his first full length novel, demonstrates an undoubted ability to tell a good story well. His earlier stories have been broadcast on Radio Scotland, and he has the rare distinction of being shortlisted for the Macallan/Scotland on Sunday Short Story Competition two years in succession.

FOLKLORE

The Supernatural Highlands

Francis Thompson
ISBN 0 946487 31 6 PBK £8.99

 An authoritative exploration of the otherworld of the Highlander, happenings and beings hitherto thought to be outwith the ordinary forces of nature. A simple introduction to the way of life of rural Highland and Island communities, this new edition weaves a path through second sight, the evil eye, witchcraft, ghosts, fairies and other supernatural beings, offering new sight-lines on areas of belief once dismissed as folklore and superstition.

Tall Tales from an Island

Peter Macnab
ISBN 0 946487 07 3 PBK £8.99
Peter Macnab was born and reared on Mull. He heard many of these tales as a lad, and others he has listened to in later years. Although collected on

Mull, they could have come from any one of the Hebridean islands. Timeless and universal, these tales are still told round the fireside when the visitors have all gone home.

There are humorous tales, grim tales, witty tales, tales of witchcraft, tales of love, tales of heroism, tales of treachery, historical tales and tales of yesteryear. There are unforgettable characters like Do'l Gorm, the philosophical roadman, and Calum nan Croig, the Gaelic storyteller whose highly developed art of convincing exaggeration mesmerised his listeners. There is a headless horseman, and a whole coven of witches. Heroes, fools, lairds, herdsmen, lovers and liars, dead men and live cats all have a place in this entrancing collection. This is a superb collection indeed, told by a master storyteller with all the rhythms remembered from the firesides of his childhood.

A popular lecturer, broadcaster and writer, Peter Macnab is the author of a number of books and articles about Mull, the island he knows so intimately and loves so much. As he himself puts it in his introduction to this book 'I am of the unswerving opinion that nowhere else in the world will you find a better way of life, nor a finer people with whom to share it.'

'*All islands, it seems, have a rich store of characters whose stories represent a kind of sub-culture without which island life would be that much poorer. Macnab has succeeded in giving the retelling of the stories a special Mull flavour, so much so that one can visualise the storytellers sitting on a bench outside the house with a few cronies, puffing on their pipes and listening with nodding approval.*' WEST HIGHLAND FREE PRESS

NATURAL SCOTLAND

Rum: Nature's Island

Magnus Magnusson

ISBN 0 946487 32 4   £7.95 PBK

Rum: Nature's Island is the fascinating story of a Hebridean island from the earliest times through to the Clearances and its period as the sporting playground of a Lancashire industrial magnate, and on to its rebirth as a National Nature Reserve, a model for the active ecological management of Scotland's wild places.

Thoroughly researched and written in a lively accessible style, the book includes comprehensive coverage of the island's geology, animals and plants, and people, with a special chapter on the Edwardian extravaganza of Kinloch Castle. There is practical information for visitors to what was once known as 'the Forbidden Isle'; the book provides details of bothy and other accommodation, walks and nature trails. It closes with a positive vision for the island's future: biologically diverse, economically dynamic and ecologically sustainable.

Rum: Nature's Island is published in co-operation with Scottish Natural Heritage (of which Magnus Magnusson is Chairman) to mark the 40th anniversary of the acquisition of Rum by its predecessor, The Nature Conservancy.

Wild Scotland: The essential guide to finding the best of natural Scotland

James McCarthy
Photography by Laurie Campbell
ISBN 0 946487 37 5 PBK £7.50

With a foreword by Magnus Magnusson and striking colour photographs by Laurie Campbell, this is the essential up-to-date guide to viewing wildlife in Scotland for the visitor and resident alike. It provides a fascinating overview of the country's plants, animals, bird and marine life against the background of their typical natural settings, as an introduction to the vivid descriptions of the most accessible localities, linked to clear regional maps. A unique feature is the focus on 'green tourism' and sustainable visitor use of the countryside, contributed by Duncan Bryden, manager of the Scottish Tourist Board's Tourism and the Environment Task Force. Important practical information on access and the best times of year for viewing sites makes this an indispensable and user-friendly travelling companion to anyone interested in exploring Scotland's remarkable natural heritage.

James McCarthy is former Deputy Director for Scotland of the Nature Conservancy Council, and now a Board Member of Scottish Natural Heritage and Chairman of the Environmental Youth Work National Development Project Scotland.

An Inhabited Solitude: Scotland – Land and People

James McCarthy
ISBN 0 946487 30 8 PBK £6.99

'Scotland is the country above all others that I have seen, in which a man of imagination may carve out his own pleasures; there are so many inhabited solitudes.'

DOROTHY WORDSWORTH, in her journal of August 1803

An informed and thought-provoking profile of Scotland's unique landscapes and the impact of humans on what we see now and in the future. James McCarthy leads us through the many aspects of the land and the people who inhabit it: natural Scotland; the rocks beneath; land ownership; the use of resources; people and place; conserving

Scottish demands for Home Rule. Knowledge of this century makes me routinely suspicious of the effective commitment to Devolution of Blair and New Labour as a whole. But putting aside such cynical mistrust of *Perfidious Albion,* I happily acknowledge that the Referendum changes everything and I should be massively grateful to it for two main reasons.

First, it provides me with a perfect finishing point for this book. That the people of Scotland should be asked their opinion about what happens to their country, by a government with a huge majority which appears to be pledged to constitutional reform, is a historical watershed whatever the result. The Referendum breaks the spell of enforced Scottish passivity which the English establishment made official in 1707. For all the reasons I outlined earlier about the emergence of a new generation of Scots, confident of their country's ability to go it alone, I am sure the Referendum will support Devolution; who knows what will happen after that? With their traditional anti-Tory *raison d'être* apparently diminished, will the hegemony of the Labour Party remain unchallenged by the SNP? Suddenly, after years of despairing of change, the immediate prospects are almost too exciting to think about.

Yet whatever comes to pass, even the unthinkable No/No majority, the Referendum is still a watershed for me. I am allowed to vote because I fulfil the residence qualifications. My second reason for being grateful to the Referendum is that it means I can play an authentic part, however tiny, in Scotland's future by voting Yes/Yes so now there's suddenly less need to wear a t-shirt or write a book.

Scotland's heritage and much more. Written in a highly readable style, this concise volume offers an understanding of the land as a whole. Emphasising the uniqueness of the Scottish environment, the author explores the links between this and other aspects of our culture as a key element in rediscovering a modern sense of the Scottish identity and perception of nationhood.

'*This book provides an engaging introduction to the mysteries of Scotland's people and landscapes. Difficult concepts are described in simple terms, providing the interested Scot or tourist with an invaluable overview of the country... It fills an important niche which, to my knowledge, is filled by no other publications.*'

BETSY KING, Chief Executive, Scottish Environmental Education Council.

Where can you find fossils on Skye?

'*...a lucid introduction to the geological record in general, a jargon-free exposition of the regional background, and a series of descriptions of specific localities of geological interest on a "trail" around the highlands.*

Having checked out the local references on the ground, I can vouch for their accuracy and look forward to investigating farther afield, informed by this guide.

Great care has been taken to explain specific terms as they occur and, in so doing, John Roberts has created a resource of great value which is eminently usable by anyone with an interest in the outdoors...the best bargain you are likely to get as a geology book in the foreseeable future.'

Jim Johnston, PRESS AND JOURNAL

WALK WITH LUATH

The Highland Geology Trail

John L Roberts

ISBN 0946487 36 7   PBK £4.99

Where can you find the oldest rocks in Europe? Where can you see ancient hills around 800 million years old? How do you tell whether a valley was carved out by a glacier, not a river? What are the Fucoid Beds? Where do you find rocks folded like putty? How did great masses of rock pile up like snow in front of a snow-plough? When did volcanoes spew lava and ash to form Skye, Mull and Rum?

Mountain Days & Bothy Nights

Dave Brown and Ian Mitchell

ISBN 0 946487 15 4 PBK £7.50

Acknowledged as a classic of mountain writing still in demand ten years after its first publication, this book takes you into the bothies, howffs and dosses on the Scottish hills. Fishgut Mac, Desperate Dan and Stumpy the Big Yin stalk hill and public house, evading gamekeepers and Royalty with a camaraderie which was the trademark of Scots hillwalking in the early days.

'The fun element comes through... how innocent the social polemic seems in our nastier world of today... the book for the rucksack this year.'
Hamish Brown, SCOTTISH MOUNTAINEERING CLUB JOURNAL

'The doings, sayings, incongruities and idiosyncrasies of the denizens of the bothy underworld... described in an easy philosophical style... an authentic word picture of this part of the climbing scene in latter-day Scotland, which, like any good picture, will increase in charm over the years.'
Iain Smart, SCOTTISH MOUNTAINEERING CLUB JOURNAL

'The ideal book for nostalgic hillwalkers of the 60s, even just the armchair and public house variety... humorous, entertaining, informative, written by two men with obvious expertise, knowledge and love of their subject.' SCOTS INDEPENDENT

'Fifty years have made no difference. Your crowd is the one I used to know... [This] must be the only complete dossers' guide ever put together.'
Alistair Borthwick, author of the immortal Always a Little Further.

The Joy of Hillwalking

Ralph Storer

ISBN 0 946487 28 6   PBK   £7.50

Apart, perhaps, from the joy of sex, the joy of hillwalking brings more pleasure to more people than any other form of human activity.

'Alps, America,

Scandinavia, you name it – Storer's been there, so why the hell shouldn't he bring all these various and varied places into his observations... [He] even admits to losing his virginity after a day on the Aggy Ridge... Well worth its place alongside Storer's earlier works.' TAC

Scotland's Mountains before the Mountaineers

Ian Mitchell

ISBN 0 946487 39 1   PBK   £9.99

How many Munros did Bonnie Prince Charlie bag?

Which clergyman climbed all the Cairngorm 4,000-ers nearly two centuries ago?

Which bandit and sheep rustler hid in the mountains while his wife saw off the sheriff officers with a shotgun?

According to Gaelic tradition, how did an outlier of the rugged Corbett Beinn Aridh Charr come to be called Spidean Moirich, 'Martha's Peak'?

Who was the murderous clansman who gave his name to Beinn Fhionnlaidh?

In this ground-breaking book, Ian Mitchell tells the story of explorations and ascents in the Scottish Highlands in the days before mountaineering became a popular sport - when bandits, Jacobites, poachers and illicit distillers traditionally used the mountains as sanctuary. The book also gives a detailed account of the map makers, road builders, geologists, astronomers and naturalists, many of whom ascended hitherto untrodden summits while working in the Scottish Highlands.

Scotland's Mountains before the Mountaineers is divided into four Highland regions, with a map of each region showing key summits. While not designed primarily as a guide, it will be a useful handbook for walkers and climbers. Based on a wealth of new research, this book offers a fresh perspective that will fascinate climbers and mountaineers and everyone interested in the history of mountaineering, cartography, the evolution of landscape and the social history of the Scottish Highlands.

LUATH WALKING GUIDES

The highly respected and continually updated guides to the Cairngorms.

'Particularly good on local wildlife and how to see it'
THE COUNTRYMAN

Walks in the Cairngorms

Ernest Cross
ISBN 0 946487 09 X PBK £3.95

This selection of walks celebrates the rare birds, animals, plants and geological wonders of a region often believed difficult to penetrate on foot. Nothing is difficult with this guide in your pocket, as Cross gives a choice for every walker, and includes valuable

tips on mountain safety and weather advice.

Ideal for walkers of all ages and skiers waiting for snowier skies.

Short Walks in the Cairngorms

Ernest Cross
ISBN 0 946487 23 5 PBK £3.95

Cross wrote this volume after overhearing a walker remark that there were no short walks for lazy ramblers in the Cairngorm region. Here is the answer: rambles through scenic woods with a welcoming pub at the end, birdwatching hints, glacier holes, or for the fit and ambitious, scrambles up hills to admire vistas of glorious scenery. Wildlife in the Cairngorms is unequalled elsewhere in Britain, and here it is brought to the binoculars of any walker who treads quietly and with respect.

SPORT

Over the Top with the Tartan Army (Active Service 1992-97)

Andrew McArthur
ISBN 0 946487 45 6 PBK £7.99

Scotland has witnessed the growth of a new and curious military phenomenon – grown men bedecked in tartan yomping across the globe, hell-bent on benevolence and ritualistic bevvying. What noble cause does this famous army serve? Why, football of course!

Taking us on an erratic world tour, McArthur gives a frighteningly funny insider's eye view of active service with the Tartan Army - the madcap antics of Scotland's travelling support in the '90s, written from the inside, covering campaigns and skirmishes from Euro '92 up to the qualifying drama for France '98 in places as diverse as Russia, the Faroes, Belarus, Sweden, Monte Carlo, Estonia, Latvia, USA and Finland.

This book is a must for any football fan who likes a good laugh.

'I commend this book to all football supporters'. Graham Spiers, SCOTLAND ON SUNDAY

'In wishing Andy McArthur all the best with this publication, I do hope he will be in a position to produce a sequel after our participation in the World Cup in France'. CRAIG BROWN, Scotland Team Coach

All royalties on sales of the book are going to Scottish charities, principally Children's Hospice Association Scotland, the only Scotland-wide charity of its kind, providing special love and care to children with terminal illnesses at its hospice, Rachel House, in Kinross.

Ski & Snowboard Scotland

Hilary Parke

ISBN 0 946487 35 9 PBK £6.99

How can you cut down the queue time and boost the snow time?
Who can show you how to cannonball the quarterpipe?
Where are the bumps that give most airtime?
Where can you watch international rugby in-between runs on the slopes?
Which mountain restaurant serves magical Mexican meals?
Which resort has the steepest on-piste run in Scotland?
Where can you get a free ski guiding service to show you the best runs?

If you don't know the answers to all these questions - plus a hundred or so more then this book is for you!

Snowsports in Scotland are still a secret treasure. There's no need to go abroad when there's such an exciting variety of terrain right here on your doorstep. You just need to know what to look for. *Ski & Snowboard Scotland* is aimed at maximising the time you have available so that the hours you spend on the snow are memorable for all the right reasons.

This fun and informative book guides you over the slopes of Scotland, giving you the inside track on all the major ski centres. There are chapters ranging from how to get there to the impact of snowsports on the environment.

'Reading the book brought back many happy memories of my early training *days at the dry slope in Edinburgh and of many brilliant weekends in the Cairngorms.'*

EMMA CARRICK-ANDERSON, from her foreword, written in the US, during a break in training for her first World Cup as a member of the British Alpine Ski Team.

SOCIAL HISTORY

A Word for Scotland

Jack Campbell
with a foreword by Magnus Magnusson
ISBN 0 946487 48 0 PBK £12.99

The inside story of a newspaper and a nation

Five tumultuous decades as they happened

'A word for Scotland' was Lord Beaverbrook's hope when he founded the *Scottish Daily Express*. That word for Scotland quickly became, and was for many years, the national newspaper of Scotland.

The pages of *A Word For Scotland* exude warmth and a wry sense of humour. Jack Campbell takes us behind the scenes to meet the larger-than-life characters and ordinary people who made and recorded the stories. Here we hear the stories behind the stories that hit the headlines in this great yarn of journalism in action.

Jack joined the infant newspaper at the age of 15 as a copy-boy. The young lad from Govan went on to become a leading player through nearly half a century of the most exciting, innovative and competitive years of the press in Scotland, finishing up as managing editor. He remembers the early days of news-gathering on a shoestring, the circulation wars, all the scoops and dramas and tragedies through nearly half a century of the most exciting, innovative and competitive years of the press in Scotland. He was with the *Scottish Daily Express* through the dramatic events of 1974 which ended the paper's long reign at 195 Albion Street, Glasgow.

It would be true to say 'all life is here'. From the Cheapside Street fire of which cost the lives of 19 Glasgow firemen, to the theft of the Stone of Destiny, to the lurid exploits of serial killer Peter Manuel, to encounters with world boxing champions Benny Lynch and Cassius Clay - this book offers telling glimpses of the characters, events, joy and tragedy which make up Scotland's story in the 20th century.

'As a rookie reporter you were proud to work on it and proud to be part of it - it was fine newspaper right at the heartbeat of Scotland.'

RONALD NEIL, Chief Executive of BBC Production, and a reporter on the *Scottish Daily Express* (1963-68)

'This book is a fascinating reminder of Scottish journalism in its heyday. It will be read avidly by those journalists who take pride in their profession – and should be compulsory reading for those who don't.'

JACK WEBSTER, columnist on *The Herald* and *Scottish Daily Express* journalist (1960-80)

'As one of the first women reporters on the Scottish Daily Express I was a pioneer on a great pioneering newspaper. It taught me a lot about life before I embarked on my career in the law.'

ISABEL SINCLAIR, QC, the second woman QC in Scotland (1964), and *Scottish Daily Express* reporter (1932-49)

The Crofting Years

Francis Thompson
ISBN 0 946487 06 5 PBK £6.95

Crofting is much more than a way of life. It is a store-house of cultural, linguistic and moral values which holds together a scattered and struggling rural population. This book fills a blank in the written history of crofting over the last two centuries. Bloody conflicts and gunboat diplomacy, treachery, compassion, music and story: all figure in this mine of information on crofting in the Highlands and Islands of Scotland.

'I would recommend this book to all who are interested in the past, but even more so to those who are interested in the future survival of our way of life and culture'
STORNOWAY GAZETTE

'A cleverly planned book... the story told in simple words which compel

attention... [by] a Gaelic speaking Lewisman with specialised knowledge of the crofting community.'*
BOOKS IN SCOTLAND

'The book is a mine of information on many aspects of the past, among them the homes, the food, the music and the medicine of our crofting forebears.'
John M Macmillan, erstwhile CROFTERS COMMISSIONER FOR LEWIS AND HARRIS

'This fascinating book is recommended to anyone who has the interests of our language and culture at heart.'
Donnie Maclean, DIRECTOR OF AN COMUNN GAIDHEALACH, WESTERN ISLES

'Unlike many books on the subject, Crofting Years combines a radical political approach to Scottish crofting experience with a ruthless realism which while recognising the full tragedy and difficulty of his subject never descends to sentimentality or nostalgia'.
CHAPMAN

MUSIC AND DANCE

Highland Balls and Village Halls

GW Lockhart
ISBN 0 946487 12 X PBK £6.95

Acknowledged as a classic in Scottish dancing circles throughout the world. Anecdotes, Scottish history, dress and dance steps are all included in this

'delightful little book, full of interest...

both a personal account and an understanding look at the making of traditions.'
NEW ZEALAND SCOTTISH COUNTRY DANCES MAGAZINE

'A delightful survey of Scottish dancing and custom. Informative, concise and opinionated, it guides the reader across the history and geography of country dance and ends by detailing the 12 dances every Scot should know – the most famous being the Eightsome Reel, "the greatest longest, rowdiest, most diabolically executed of all the Scottish country dances".'
THE HERALD

'A pot-pourri of every facet of Scottish country dancing. It will bring back memories of petronella turns and poussettes and make you eager to take part in a Broun's reel or a dashing white sergeant!'
DUNDEE COURIER AND ADVERTISER

'An excellent an very readable insight into the traditions and customs of Scottish country dancing. The author takes us on a tour from his own early days jigging in the village hall to the characters and traditions that have made our own brand of dance popular throughout the world.'
SUNDAY POST

Fiddles & Folk: A celebration of the re-emergence of Scotland's musical heritage

GW Lockhart
ISBN 0 946487 38 3 PBK £7.95

In *Fiddles & Folk*, his companion volume to *Highland Balls and Village*

Halls, now an acknowledged classic on Scottish dancing, Wallace Lockhart meets up with many of the people who have created the renaissance of Scotland's music at home and overseas.

From Dougie MacLean, Hamish Henderson, the Battlefield Band, the Whistlebinkies, the Scottish Fiddle Orchestra, the McCalmans and many more come the stories that break down the musical barriers between Scotland's past and present, and between the diverse musical forms which have woven together to create the dynamism of the music today.

'I have tried to avoid a formal approach to Scottish music as it affects those of us with our musical heritage coursing through our veins. The picture I have sought is one of many brush strokes, looking at how some individuals have come to the fore, examining their music, lives, thoughts, even philosophies...'
WALLACE LOCKHART

' "I never had a narrow, woolly-jumper, fingers stuck in the ear approach to music. We have a musical heritage here that is the envy of the rest of the world. Most countries just can't compete," he [Ian Green, Greentrax] says. And as young Scots tire of Oasis and Blur, they will realise that there is a wealth of young Scottish music on their doorstep just waiting to be discovered.' THE SCOTSMAN, March 1998

For anyone whose heart lifts at the sound of fiddle or pipes, this book takes you on a delightful journey, full of humour and respect, in the company of some of the performers who have taken Scotland's music around the world and come back enriched.

HISTORY

On the Trail of William Wallace

David R. Ross

ISBN 0 946487 47 2 PBK £7.99

How close to reality was *Braveheart*?

Where was Wallace actually born?

What was the relationship between Wallace and Bruce?

Are there any surviving eye-witness accounts of Wallace?

How does Wallace influence the psyche of today's Scots?

On the Trail of William Wallace offers a refreshing insight into the life and heritage of the great Scots hero whose proud story is at the very heart of what it means to be Scottish. Not concentrating simply on the hard historical facts of Wallace's life, the book also takes into account the real significance of Wallace and his effect on the ordinary Scot through the ages, manifested in the many sites where his memory is marked.

In trying to piece together the jigsaw of the reality of Wallace's life, David Ross weaves a subtle flow of new information with his own observa-tions. His engaging, thoughtful and at times amusing narrative reads with the ease of a historical novel, complete with all the intrigue, treachery and romance required to hold the attention of the casual reader and still entice the more knowledgable historian.

74 places to visit in Scotland and the north of England

One general map and 3 location maps

Stirling and Falkirk battle plans

Wallace's route through London

Chapter on Wallace connections in North America and elsewhere

Reproductions of rarely seen illustrations

On the Trail of William Wallace will be enjoyed by anyone with an interest in Scotland, from the passing tourist to the most fervent nationalist. It is an encyclopaedia-cum-guide book, literally stuffed with fascinating titbits not usually on offer in the conventional history book.

David Ross is organiser of and historical adviser to the Society of William Wallace.

'*Historians seem to think all there is to be known about Wallace has already been uncovered. Mr Ross has proved that Wallace studies are in fact in their infancy.*' ELSPETH KING, Director the the Stirling Smith Art Museum & Gallery, who annotated and introduced the recent Luath edition of *Blind Harry's Wallace*.

'*Better the pen than the sword!*' RANDALL WALLACE, author of *Braveheart*, when asked by David Ross how it felt to be partly responsible for the freedom of a nation following the Devolution Referendum.

POETRY

Blind Harry's Wallace

William Hamilton of Gilbertfield

ISBN 0 946487 43 X HBK £15.00
ISBN 0 946487 33 2 PBK £7.50

The original story of the real braveheart, Sir William Wallace. Racy, blood on every page, violently a n g l o - p h o b i c, grossly embellished, vulgar and disgusting, clumsy and stilted, a literary failure, a great epic.

Whatever the verdict on BLIND HARRY, this is the book which has done more than any other to frame the notion of Scotland's national identity. Despite its numerous 'historical inaccuracies', it remains the principal source for what we now know about the life of Wallace.

The novel and film *Braveheart* were based on the 1722 Hamilton edition of this epic poem. Burns, Wordsworth, Byron and others were greatly influenced by this version 'wherein the old obsolete words are rendered more intelligible', which is said to be the book, next to the Bible, most commonly found in Scottish households in the eighteenth century. Burns even admits to having 'borrowed... a couplet worthy of Homer' directly from Hamilton's version of BLIND HARRY to include in 'Scots wha hae'.

Elspeth King, in her introduction to this, the first accessible edition of BLIND HARRY in verse form since 1859, draws parallels between the situation in Scotland at the time of Wallace and that in Bosnia and Chechnya in the 1990s. Seven hundred years to the day after the Battle of Stirling Bridge, the 'Settled Will of the Scottish People' was expressed in the devolution referendum of 11 September 1997. She describes this as a landmark opportunity for mature reflection on how the nation has been shaped, and sees BLIND HARRY'S WALLACE as an essential and compelling text for this purpose.

'Builder of the literary foundations of a national hero-cult in a free and powerful country'.

ALEXANDER STODDART, sculptor

'A true bard of the people'.

TOM SCOTT, THE PENGUIN BOOK OF SCOTTISH VERSE, on Blind Harry.

'A more inventive writer than Shakespeare'.

RANDALL WALLACE

'The story of Wallace poured a Scottish prejudice in my veins which will boil along until the floodgates of life shut in eternal rest'.

ROBERT BURNS

'Hamilton's couplets are not the best poetry you will ever read, but they rattle along at a fair pace. In re-issuing this work, the publishers have re-opened the

spring from which most of our
conceptions of the Wallace legend come'.

SCOTLAND ON SUNDAY

'The return of Blind Harry's Wallace, a
man who makes Mel look like a wimp'.

THE SCOTSMAN

Poems to be read aloud

Collected and with an introduction by
Tom Atkinson
ISBN 0 946487 00 6 PBK £5.00

 This personal col-
lection of doggerel
and verse ranging
from the tear-jerking
Green Eye of the Yellow
God to the rarely
printed,   bawdy
Eskimo Nell has a
lively cult following.
Much borrowed and rarely returned,
this is a book for reading aloud in very
good company, preferably after a dram
or twa. You are guaranteed a warm
welcome if you arrive at a gathering
with this little volume in your pocket.
'This little book is an attempt to stem the
great rushing tide of canned
entertainment. A hopeless attempt of
course. There is poetry of very high order
here, but there is also some fearful
doggerel. But that is the way of things. No
literary axe is being ground.
Of course some of the items in this book
are poetic drivel, if read as poems. But
that is not the point. They all spring to life
when they are read aloud. It is the
combination of the poem with your voice,
with all the art and craft you can muster,
that produces the finished product and
effect you seek.

You don't have to learn the poems. Why
clutter up your mind with rubbish? Of
course, it is a poorly furnished mind that
doesn't carry a fair stock of poetry, but
surely the poems to be remembered and
savoured in secret, when in love, or ill, or
sad, are not the ones you want to share
with an audience.
So go ahead, clear your throat and
transfix all talkers with a stern eye, then
let rip!

TOM ATKINSON

Luath Press Limited
committed to publishing well written books worth reading

LUATH PRESS takes its name from Robert Burns, whose little collie Luath (*Gael.*, swift or nimble) tripped up Jean Armour at a wedding and gave him the chance to speak to the woman who was to be his wife and the abiding love of his life. Burns called one of *The Twa Dogs* Luath after Cuchullin's hunting dog in *Ossian's Fingal*. Luath Press grew up in the heart of Burns country, and now resides a few steps up the road from Burns' first lodgings in Edinburgh's Royal Mile.
Luath offers you distinctive writing with a hint of unexpected pleasures.

Most UK bookshops either carry our books in stock or can order them for you. To order direct from us, please send a £sterling cheque, postal order, international money order or your credit card details (number, address of cardholder and expiry date) to us at the address below. Please add post and packing as follows: UK – £1.00 per delivery address; overseas surface mail – £2.50 per delivery address; overseas airmail – £3.50 for the first book to each delivery address, plus £1.00 for each additional book by airmail to the same address. If your order is a gift, we will happily enclose your card or message at no extra charge.

Luath Press Limited
543/2 Castlehill
The Royal Mile
Edinburgh EH1 2ND
Telephone: 0131 225 4326 (24 hours)
Fax: 0131 225 4324
email: gavin.macdougall@luath.co.uk
Website: www.luath.co.uk